Ghost Stories:

Chilling True Tales of Ghosts

Steph Young

Introduction

Chilling True Tales of Ghosts From bestselling author Steph Young.

A collection of the rarest and most chilling true ghost stories around.

Here follows accounts of ghosts who seek deadly revenge upon the living, of twisted tortured souls who return to hound those who are still mortal....

Table of Contents

Chapter One:

The Red Barn

An infamous tale of betrayal, murder, and supernatural revenge, the tale of the Red Barn Murder encompasses treacherous double lives, a vengeful ghost, a book made of human skin, and a hanging so popular that tickets had to be issued.

The true events took place in 1828 in the small rural village of Polstead, in Suffolk, England. The tale became so popular that the village became a ghoulish tourist attraction at the time, with several hundred thousand visitors descending on it in one year alone. Across the country, Fairground peep shows created new apertures for visitors to watch a grisly re-enactment of the murder.

Planks of wood were stolen by visitors to 'the Red Barn,' and pieces of rope used to hang the murderer were sold for a guinea. A lock of the murdered woman's hair was sold for 2 guineas. Part of the killer's scalp and one ear were placed on display in a shop in the busiest retail street in London; Oxford Street, and tiny pieces of the 'Red Barn' were sold as toothpicks.

The story features an unmarried woman, Maria Marten, who'd had several children out of wedlock – something quite scandalous in those days, that could even lead to arrest, and it was a situation which often led to destitution and a desperate existence, with some women in this position trying to do all they could to make a better life and marry well; few would succeed however, as once in this position of illegitimacy, eligible men would not want to involve themselves.

The saga began when Maria suddenly vanished, and her father began receiving letters from her, telling him she had moved to the Isle of Wight with a local farmer's son, to start a new life. Her father couldn't understand why she wouldn't have told him this, but she sounded happy and settled there, with William 'Foxey' Corder; although it was Corder who penned the letters rather than Maria herself, as Corder explained in the letters that Maria had hurt her hand, or was temporarily under the weather, or, when her father asked him why she did not write directly herself, he explained that her letters must surely have got lost in the post.

Then, after a few months had passed, with the letters still continuing, her father's wife, Maria's step-mother Ann, began to have very unsettling dreams, in which she saw her husband's daughter dead and buried in an outdoor building that in her visions looked very much like a local barn; called the 'Red Barn.' She was having very vivid and very realistic visions of her step-daughter dead in the barn; so vivid that she felt these were not dreams at all but visitations by the ghost of her step-daughter who was communicating with her, showing her where she had been killed and buried.

The nightly visitations by the ghost so disturbed her step-mother that in the end, she confided in her husband and told him they must go to the Red Barn; that if they did, they would find his daughter dead. Her father agreed to do this, to soothe and pacify his wife, and soon a dig of the Red Barn began.

It was not long before the body of his daughter was indeed unearthed in the Red Barn. Ann Martin would later testify in court about the visitations of her step-daughter's ghost which had led to the digging up of the Red Barn. When her body was found, Maria was recognisable from her clothes and her hair and the gap in her teeth, although decomposition had set in. Tied around her neck was one of William's handkerchiefs. She had not been in the Isle of Wight then; despite the letters, all written by 'Foxey' Corder.

Local famer's son William Corder had been given the nickname 'Foxey' when in school, due to his reputation for sharp intelligence but slyness too and local gossip had it that he did not necessarily always act within the boundaries of the law. It was said that he'd tried to pass a forged cheque and had sold his father's pigs without the required license. In fact, how much was really true isn't known but it was believed that when younger, his father had sent him to London to join the Navy.

Due to poor eye-sight however, he failed the entry test. Rather than returning home to his village in Suffolk, Corder attempted to make a living in London and became involved with a petty gang of criminals including prostitute Hannah 'Fandango' who came from the same village and the leader of the gang, a man called "Beauty," but legally named Sam Smith.

Corder's attempts to live-by-crime was unsuccessful however, and he returned to the village when his father agreed he could come back. Shortly after this, during a hard winter, his father and two of his brothers became ill with tuberculosis. The two brothers recovered only just and were permanently disabled by the effects of the devastating disease, while his father succumbed to it and died. The eldest son, who had been unaffected, now inherited the farm. It was around this time that Maria Marten caught William's eye. He was known to be a ladies man and a woman-chaser, and Maria in some respects had a similar reputation, although in those days of course, she was greatly stigmatised as a fallen women of wanton behaviour.

She'd actually already had an illegitimate child by Corder's own brother Thomas. This had been hushed up and the infant had died too, as was common in an era of such poverty and harsh living conditions. Maria then had a second illegitimate child born by a relationship with the son of landed gentry. This man's social position was higher than William's and again, the affair was hushed up, although the child's father Peter Mathews did send monthly payments to her for the child's upkeep – as long as she agreed to stay out of his life!

Her next affair had been with William Corder; the man who had written letters to her father from the Isle of Wight. Of course, she had not been in the Isle of Wight and he had only been there momentarily, long enough to write the letters and post them. Then she was found dead in the Red Barn and he'd turned up in London town again, living with another woman. He'd met this new woman after placing an advert in the Lonely Heart's section of the Times Newspaper, while Maria lay undiscovered and buried under the Red Barn.

Maria and Corder's affair had been a low-key

relationship, kept mostly secret from the village. They'd met at secluded and isolated spots only, including the Red Barn. Once more, Maria had fallen pregnant and as the pregnancy progressed, she was unable to keep it a secret. William said he would marry her once the child was born, at least according to Maria's father. In fact, the child died 3 weeks after it was born. William and Maria then decided to bury the child in secret.

At the time, Maria could have faced a public whipping – for the crime of having children out of wedlock. Indeed, one day, William came to her and urged her to leave the village – he said he'd heard rumours that the Parish Officers were planning to have her arrested – or were they?

William duly arranged that they must meet at the Red Barn and run away together and get married. They duly ran off, it was supposed, and yet in reality, days later, William returned alone. He told her father that there'd been an issue with the marriage license and that she was waiting in Ipswich for it to be sorted out. William was now running the farm – his elder brother had recently died by drowning when he'd fallen through ice as he'd tried to cross a lake.

William remained at the farm for a number of weeks, then informed Maria's father that he would be travelling to the Isle of Wight, where he said Maria had gone. Days later, her father began to receive letters from his daughter, written, little did he know, by William not Maria. The first letter informed her father that the couple had now married, and that William was going to sell the farm and set up a new business on the Isle of Wight.

That winter was when Ann Martin, Maria's step-mother, started to find her night-times besieged by the ghost of her step-daughter, imploring her to go to the Red Barn. The 'dreams' at night were so realistic that Ann became convinced Maria was buried under the floor of the Red Barn, situated on the land of William's farm.

Her husband, who incidentally had a rather curious profession of making a living by catching moles and turning them into gloves! agreed to find out. He went to the man running the farm in William's absence and asked for permission to enter the Red barn. With him, went Maria's step-mother and she led them to a precise spot inside the barn.

Suspiciously, at this spot, the ground looked as though it had been disturbed. Maria's father used one of his mole-catching spikes and struck it into the ground. When he pulled it back out, decomposing flesh was attached to it. A witness would later come forward to say they'd seen William walking toward the barn with a pickaxe in his hand.

How she'd died could not be determined, but obviously, the prime suspect was William. He was discovered by police in London. He was living with the woman he'd met through the lonely-hearts column of The Times Newspaper and was helping her run a Boarding House for young ladies, (other accounts say it was a girl's school) and in fact, he'd married her. His new wife was a former school teacher. However, police discovered a passport in his name along with plans to travel alone to France! The police believed he was plotting to leave the country before Maria's body ended up being found. He had pistols too. London policemen James Lea gained access to William's new residence by pretending to be the father of a daughter he wished to board there. William was arrested and taken away.

When he was arrested, he denied all knowledge of his former lover's murder. Word soon spread of the discovery of the woman in the Red Barn and the accused man, and the public became gripped as the Newspapers salaciously described the grisly and scandalous details of the couple, with its heady mix of illicit love, murder and supernatural messages. Hundreds attended her funeral.

At the subsequent murder trial, the judiciary even struggled to find suitable jurors who had not already read about all the juicy details in the Newspapers and formed their opinion of William's guilt. The huge number of people wishing to attend the trial led to every hostelry in the town being fully booked and tickets had to be issued for attendees, in order to ensure crowding did not become a safety issue.

The prosecution sought to persuade the jury that William had wanted rid of Maria and her damaged reputation and they painted an image of him as a black sheep and criminal, because of his past associations. They suggested that Maria had been blackmailing him – and that in a desperate effort to be free of her, he had shot then stabbed her to death.

Maria's brother gave evidence that he knew William's gun was loaded before Maria had disappeared. She had been shot in the cheek. William said she had accidently been shot in the eye as she was changing out of men's clothes; he'd told her to dress up as a man to elude Parish Police who may be out looking for her to arrest her for her 'crime' of bearing illicit children.

However, she had also been stabbed in the ribs – unless that wound had been caused by her father's mole-catching implement when he'd struck it in the ground perhaps. However, there was also a stab wound on her neck. She'd also quite possibly been strangled too – presumably with William's handkerchief found still tied around her neck. Certainly, it looked like over-kill. A crime of passion? Had they argued terribly and things had escalated? Or, could even someone else have put William in the frame? There were rumours, unproven of course and unsubstantiated, and perhaps wicked gossip, but the rumours were that Maria's step-mother, who was only a couple of years older than Maria, had developed feelings for William.

On the other hand, the defence team claimed that Maria had killed herself after arguing with William and that he had merely panicked and hidden her body. The jury took just over ½ an hour to find him guilty – and the judge ordered him to be hung until dead. While awaiting the death sentence to be carried out, William made a confession; he said he had killed Maria but this had been a tragic accident. He said he had shot her by accident when she was changing out of the men's clothes she'd been wearing. He said he did not stab her. It was too late now however; he'd already been condemned to die.

He was put to death in front of an enormous crowd, estimated at up to 20,000 people, who had all clambered to watch. Once he was dead, his body was left hanging on the scaffold for a while, for people to look at, then he was transported to the county hall where he was put on display with his stomach cut open, for some reason. Thousands queued to view him. The hangman sold off pieces of the rope used to hang him. The Red Barn was eventually pulled down but not before many curious members of the public had travelled there to steal pieces of the barn as souvenirs.

William's body was used for a dissection demonstration to medical students, while his skull was either stolen or sold, ending up in the hands of a Dr John Kilner who also had one of his ears. The story goes that after the doctor took ownership of the skull, any candles in the same room, would never stay lit - they would constantly be snuffed out somehow. Dr. Kilner was a general practitioner and one evening his maid told him a man had come for a late appointment at the surgery.

When the doctor left his office and went into the waiting room to ask the man to come into his office to see him, the room was empty – yet he felt the distinct sensation of a shadow in the dark room, as if a presence was there. He enquired from his maid if she had imagined a man had called at the front door because the room was now empty, but she insisted she had let a man in. Puzzled, the Doctor shrugged it off and went back to his office.

A few days later, he watched his door handle turn when he was quite alone in the house. Determined to find out who was behind the door, he rushed to open it but found the hallway empty. He made his way to the front door, but on opening it he was assaulted by a violent gust of wind that nearly knocked him off his feet. After a number of continued unsettlingly spooky incidents, he decided to rid himself of the skull, convinced that, although a skeptic and rational scientist, that the spirit of the hanged man was haunting him.

He took the skull and gave it to the Jailer where William had been hung, who it is said also went on to experience bad luck and ill fortune. Eventually the skull was taken to a Priest, and it was given a proper Christian burial. Dr. Kilner had also taken possession of

William's scalp, which had come attached to one of his ears, but this eventually ended up at Suffolk's Moyses Hall Museum, along with the curious display of a book written about an account of the murder, which had been bound with William's skin.

The story lived on for many decades, with plays, ballads, and poems all written of the tale, and many melodramatic newspaper stories entertaining audiences in true Penny Dreadful style.

Chapter Two:

The Ghost's Revenge

In a treacherous tale of infamy, deceit and betrayal, according to account of 1631, the ghost the ghost of a murdered girl came back to reap deadly revenge upon an assassin and the man who had hired him to kill her.

Ann Walker was a young woman who had been hired by a wealthy widower to work as his housekeeper, in the village of Lumley, near Chester-Le-Street, in the county of Durham, England. Perhaps inevitably, they became very close and soon Ann fell pregnant. As the pregnancy became harder to conceal, few in the village doubted who the father could be and William Walker, the widower, did not want his reputation ruined any further by the brewing scandal of his behaviour. You see, Ann was actually his niece – he'd entered into an incestuous union with his own niece and the scandal would have been awful.

That March, he decided he must take action. He told Ann he was sending her away until after the baby was born. He told her he would look after her and provide for the baby, but she could not give birth to it in his house. At first, he sent her to live with her aunt, then he told villagers she had gone to live in the city of Durham. A couple of weeks passed, and the villagers were surprised not to have heard from Ann herself. She was well-known in the village and her absence was noted. She was an attractive young woman who, by all accounts, had been devoted to her uncle.

The saga of her ghost began when, not longer after this, local farmer James Graham was busy at work late after midnight in his mill, working by candlelight to make flour after the year's harvest had been plentiful. Every night, he would work in the mill alone, sometimes whistling happily as he worked. He was glad to have a good bounty to sell to feed his family. But one night, he felt a terrible shiver come over him as the mill suddenly became ice cold.

With this sudden cold came a dreadful feeling of

eeriness, as though everything had suddenly stopped, and an unsettling quiet filled the room. Out of the corner of his eye, he became aware that he was not alone. Standing close-by was a hideous, ghastly apparition of a woman with blood pouring from severe wounds in her head. The blood was pouring down her face and over her peasant dress. Her eyes were fixed on Graham with an expression of torment.

In The Antiquities of the county of Palatine of Durham from 1816 Robert Surtees writes; 'There stood a woman, with her hair about her head, hanging down, and all bloody, with several large wounds on her head.' The miller, 'being much affrighted, began to bless himself; and at last asked her what she wanted?'

She began to speak; 'I am the spirit of Ann Walker. I have been murdered. I lived with your neighbour John Walker. Being got with child by him, he promised to send me to a private place where I should be well looked to, then I should come again to his house.'

'But I was betrayed by him. I was told to go with a Mark

Sharpe, a collier, who upon a moor slew me with a pick, and after, threw my body into a coal pit. Walker paid him. He couldn't get the blood off his shoes and clothes, so he hid them as well. If you do not tell about this crime, I will haunt you forever." Her eyes bore into him with such fierceness and anger.

This ghastly figure told the miller that the widower, her uncle, had paid this assassin to kill her, and she'd been smashed in the skull by his pickaxe. Her own uncle, her flesh and blood, had used her in the worst way possible – he had ordered her to be killed and had not even got his own hands dirty.

As for the killer, her blood had splashed all over his clothes – she'd been struck in the head at least five times with the axe, and although he had tried to wash the blood out in the nearby River Wear, in the end, he had stripped off, thrown his clothes and shoes down the mine shaft on top of her dead body, and fled half-naked from the murder scene. She told the terrified miller she wanted vengeance. He must tell the authorities.

Then she disappeared. The miller had to sit down from the shock. He was alone again, but he was shaking from the sight of her awful eyes, her terrible head wounds, and the anger in her voice. Could he have imagined it? Was he over-tired and his imagination had sent a hideous vision like a living-nightmare? He struggled to carry on that night and quite quickly he found himself shutting up the barn and hurrying back to the safety of his farmhouse nearby.

When he got into bed, he could not settle – the pitiful sight of the woman and the fire in her angry eyes was haunting him. It was light by the time he finally drifted off.

The next morning, he gave himself a good shake and resolved to put last night out of his mind – it was beyond belief that a ghost had come to his barn, and he determined to say nothing to his wife and family, let alone the authorities, despite the ghost imploring him to. The miller was also fully aware that he could not simply go around making accusations against the widower, who was wealthy and of far higher standing in the community than he.

The following night, the apparition did not come to him when he worked again in his barn. His relief was palpable; but it did not last. His wife noticed that her husband appeared quieter, subdued, and she asked him what was wrong, but he would not tell her. A few nights later, he was in bed asleep with his wife when he suddenly woke to the sensation of the sheet being lifted from his body and ice-cold covering him. He opened his eyes to find the ghost of bloody Marie had returned.

Again, blood was pouring down her face and onto her clothes and this time, her eyes were filled with tears. She was sobbing, begging him to go to the authorities – to tell them that she had been viciously, savagely axed to death by a hired killer; that her employer, the widower, had wickedly betrayed her. She became fierce and threatening, and she cruelly told the miller she would never stop haunting him; she would be relentless.

Once more, the next morning the miller tried to put it

out of his mind – it was just a nightmare, he told himself. He must stop letting his imagination run riot and get on with his work. Besides which; who would believe such a ridiculous tale of nonsense and superstition, of ghosts and ghouls. But that night, as he returned to the farmhouse through the woods, she appeared to him again.

She warned him that she would plague him for eternity if he did not do as she asked. The miller felt he could no longer bear to see her hideous bloody wounds and the fire in her eyes; he did not want to see her ever again, and so this time he did do as she implored him to. The very next morning he took himself to the Magistrate and he started to explain what had been happening to him.

At first, the Magistrate tried to shrug him off; but Walker could not be pacified, and he persisted, insisting this was real; she really was haunting him, and the magistrate must take action. Eventually, the magistrate consented to send a party of men to investigate the mine shaft where the ghost of Ann said she had been murdered and thrown down. To the astonishment of all concerned, there lying at the bottom of the pit was the horrifically wounded dead body of Ann Walker and a pile of blood-stained men's clothes.

The magistrate issued the order for the arrests of the widower William Walker and his hired killer Mark Sharp and they were quickly seized. They were both charged with her murder. Mark Sharp, the killer, a close friend of her uncle, had visited Ann's aunt where she had first been sent to live, and told her that her uncle (and lover) had arranged for her to be accommodated in a house far away from the county, away from idle gossip of the villagers, and she must go with him; but instead, Sharp had lured her to the mine shaft, struck her with the axe multiple times and killed her.

With little other evidence than the bloody clothes, both the widower and the hired killer were found guilty by a jury in the trial at Durham Assizes in August 1632, and Ann's body was given a Christian burial in consecrated ground.

During their trial, at which both prisoners pleaded not guilty, the judge himself saw the ghost of Ann standing behind the widower in court, and the foreman of the jury said he saw her ghost upon the shoulders of Walker, her killer, as did a member of the jury too; both of them said that she looked very young. The widower and his hired killer were hung, despite them continuing to plead their innocence, even when standing on the gallows.

Chapter Three:

Cursed

The curious case of Christopher Case; In April 1991, Christopher Case was Director of Programming for Muzak, the Company responsible for introducing elevator music and department store jingles. Growing up, he'd always had a passion for music. He grew up in Richmond, Virginia, and was known by all his friends and family for his love of music as well as for being a fitness fanatic. He'd been a DJ back then and had often preferred listening to music, rather than socializing and going out at night.

The worst anyone could say about him was that he was sometimes a bit of a loner. A good friend from his DJ days in Richmond, Sammy Saddo said, "One of the reason's I get emotional about it is because he was my friend and I loved him, and I didn't like the way he died. He would travel around the world with his job, so he didn't date much but women liked him. He was the kind of guy you could rely on – everybody's friend."

Fast forward to the night he died; on the night Christopher Case died, he had almost resigned himself to his fate. He had accepted that his death would most likely come. He felt that he simply would not be able to stop it, and although he put up a fight, his fears were confirmed. He did not make it through the night. He was found clothed in a kneeling position, dead, surrounded by crosses and crucifixes and salt. The candles he had lit had burned-down. He had no wounds. Soft religious music was still playing in the background. He had prepared himself for the battle; but he had lost.

One of the reporters who covered the story was Lewis Course for the Seattle Times. "What intrigued me was the fact that from everything I knew from what I'd been told about it, he was pretty level-headed." Nobody who knew him can understand the week in the summer of '91 that ended in such tragedy.

It all began when he'd gone on a business trip to San Francisco. A male business friend had introduced him to a woman who was importing rare music from Egypt.

She had some information on ancient Egyptian music and of course, music was his life, so he was very interested in that, but Christopher would later say there was something very strange about the dark-haired woman.

She had a special intensity about her, he said. It was obvious to Christopher that she wanted to start a relationship with him. She was older than he was, and she was, in his opinion, quickly enamoured of him, and he didn't like that at all. He had no interest whatsoever other than the ancient Egyptian music she knew so much about.

The second time they met, to continue discussing the Egyptian music was in a restaurant. She came on even stronger to Case that night, he later told his close friends, and he said he pulled away from her, telling her it was time they left. This greatly angered her, and she uttered something strange to him; she said that she was a witch and that he would be very sorry. She told him she was going to put a curse on him.

Christopher returned home from his business trip to San Francisco and for a time he dismissed the incident from his mind, the way most rational people would. He mentioned it to his friend Sammy, but he didn't sound alarmed when he first told her. He said, this lady I met, she said she's a witch and Sammy said she told him, "Just bless her and go on about your business."

This was the first of 3 calls and the calls would become increasingly worse until the night of Wednesday 17th April 1990, when he would find himself in a mortal battle for his life. It had been less than a week since his meeting with this mystery woman, who described herself as a witch. He had not heard from the woman again after leaving San Francisco; yet, "It seemed that his encounters with her were beginning to play on his mind, and it was horrible," said Sammi.

"I wish someone could hear what I heard in his voice, and what he said; it was a living hell. It's my understanding that he would try to sleep but he had gotten to the point that he was not sleeping."

On the Tuesday, Christopher visited a religious book store called Evangeline Inc, not far from his apartment. The Store manager, Rodney Higuchi took particular notice of Christopher as he entered the store. Christopher asked him where the Crosses were. "Then I saw him collect quite a few in his hands so I asked him what he was going to be using them for and he mentioned at that time that he was battling some supernatural forces and he wanted them for protection. He wanted to know if they had been blessed with holy water.

"I just don't know what to do now," Christopher told the Store manager. "I can't sleep." He returned from the Store and scattered the crosses and crucifixes throughout his apartment and he spread salt in the corners of every room.

Later that day, he phoned his friend Sammi again. "It's like they're putting thoughts in my head before I can even think them," he told her. "They've attacked me in the middle of the night." He told her had woken up to find small cuts on his fingers. He was terrified. He hadn't shown up for work in two days. He sat and wrote notes on methods of combating evil spirits. He told his worried friends that he believed the curse was taking hold of him. That night, he became so terrified that he felt he could not remain in his apartment. He left and checked into a hotel nearby.

When he returned to his apartment the next day, he wrote more notes on rituals he could do to fight the powers of darkness that were so violently besieging him. He lined the base of each wall with more salt, and he fashioned a geometric pattern in salt at the front door. He spread copious amounts of salt in large piles in every corner of each room.

He returned to the spiritual Bookstore Store once more. This time, the Bookstore owner felt that he was seeing a changed man. Mr Higuchi said, "When he first came in, he wasn't very agitated, and nothing looked out of the ordinary. When he came in the 2nd time, he looked exhausted and worn out and then I realized that it was affecting him more than just mentally, I mean, it was a physical thing he was going through. When I talked with him on that Wednesday morning, my feeling was he was ready to die, because he said to me, he said; "You know, I can die from this."

Shortly after 8pm that night, Sammy Souder called the Seattle police with grave concerns that Case had not answered her calls all day. Homicide Detective Larry Peterson King Kelly said police initially received information to warrant a welfare check at chase's apartment prior to the night of his death. They found his apartment door locked and had received no response from knocking on his door.

They noticed a line of salt outside his front door. They felt they had no reason to break down his door however, as they did not think the welfare call was an emergency call. Neighbours would later tell the homicide detective that Christopher Case was a very private man.

After Christopher's second trip to the Bookstore, he also visited a Priest, apparently in a desperate state. Father Janes Mallahan later told the TV show 'The

Extraordinary,' that he'd been disturbed by the man's condition. He could tell Christopher Case was scared to death and that his terror was greatly affecting his physical condition as well as his mind. The Priest said Chase asked him for advice on how to combat supernatural forces. He was in great fear that he was going to be killed.

That evening, his friend Sammy returned home to find an ansaphone message on her phone from Christopher. It was the last time she heard his voice. "Oh well, they just about got me," he said in the message. The most chilling aspect of it, she said, was the total acceptance of his fate; his total resignation to his impending death.

The next day, all her calls to him went unanswered. At 3.38pm that afternoon, the police entered his apartment. It was a mess. There were scribbled notes everywhere. The floor was littered with his writing and covered with piles of Salt.

"I heard religious music playing on the radio from the living room," said the homicide detective. A flicker of light came through the bathroom doorway. As the officers entered, they came across the final frozen moment of Christopher Case's life. The candles had burned down. He was kneeling in prayer. "I saw the victim slumped over on his knees with his head resting on the edge of the tub, left of the faucet."

He was in the bathtub, fully clothed. "A trickle of cold water ran from the tap. He was still wearing his glasses. He had died sometime during the night. The Seattle coroner officially ruled the cause of death as cardiac arrest; but those who knew him, especially during the final week of his life, knew there was a lot more to his demise.

'Heart Failure Killed Man Who Feared `Curse,' wrote the local Newspaper. The cause of death was acute myocarditis, said Rich Garner, a medical investigator with the King County Medical Examiner's office. Myocarditis is an inflammation of the heart muscle.

"I firmly believe he died of fright. He was scared to death literally," said his friend Sammi. The Seattle

Times wrote; 'Mystery Death of North Kingston Man whose body was found surrounded by occult symbols." The report describes the death scene as taking place in the bathtub. 'There was no evidence of foul play, but the presence of crucifixes and piles of salt throughout the apartment have baffled investigators. Kings County Police Major Jackson said the salt and other objects at the scene have some significance in self-protection against demons or evil spirits.'

King County Police Major Jackson Beard said, on discovery of the body, "At this point, this is a suspicious death; something that need to be explained." But he added, "I don't believe there was any foul play – this could be suicide or natural death or there was something else going on here."

He said he was waiting on toxicology results. They later came back clean. Case didn't smoke, hardly drank and did not take drugs. Sammy Souder believes that her friend may have died from fright. Souder said she had known Christopher for 10 years and that he had always been stable; until a week earlier. "People are trying to do things to me," he told her in the first phone call. He left the same message with another close female friend. "He was frantic," said Souder.

On April 14th, the first of three phone calls, Christopher called her claiming to be up all night hearing whispering voices that he could not find the source of; he felt as though he was being watched and would see moving shadows within the apartment that night. In a series of ever increasingly desperate phone calls, he told her. "They've attacked me in the middle of the night." He told her had woken up to find small cuts on his fingers. He was terrified. "It's like they're putting thoughts in my head before I can even think them."

Did Christopher Case simply die from a very rare inflammation of the heart? Or did the whispering voices and the shadowy figures he saw in his apartment result in his death? Had the witch sent evil spirits to destroy him, as she had promised? He had never been under a doctor for a heart problem. He was a fitness enthusiast and had never noticed a problem with his heart. He looked after himself well – he didn't smoke, he barely drank, he didn't take drugs.

He'd never had time off work for illness – until that last week of his life, when the terror of what was being unleashed upon him became too much for his mind, according to his closest friends. Surely, if Christopher had a potentially fatal underlying heart condition, is it not an incredible coincidence that it happened to rear its head just in the week that he was in mortal fear for his life? Did Christopher Case die of fright?

That final night he set up his defence lines about midnight. He had the meticulous care of a man who believed every placement of his candles and salt and crosses and religious writing could be the difference between victory and defeat. By now, Christopher Case had come to believe he might somehow survive the night only by encircling himself with religious items that would fight off the evil spirits.

After carefully positioning eight large candles around the perimeter of his bathtub, he placed crucifixes and crosses between each candle while soft religious music filled the rooms of his apartment. He lit the candles then climbed in his empty bathtub fully clothed, to wait out the night.

"I'm in trouble Sammi, I'm in deep trouble," he said in his last phone call. What really happened to Christopher Case on the last night of his life? Was he in a battle for his very soul? Did a witch's spell really kill him? Is it entirely possible that an ancient Egyptian curse or spell really was unleashed by this mysterious and intense woman he had met, who claimed to be a witch?

Dr. Stephen Skinner is a scholar of ancient Egyptian magic and has dedicated much of his life to the restoration and interpretation of the most ancient texts on magic and ancient spells from the Greco-Egyptian period. He is one of the leading authorities on classical magic and the grimoires of old and magical writings. Many of his books bring these ancient magic texts to the English-speaking world for the first time. Ancient Egyptian magic and spells, it seems, comes from ancient Greek Magic.

"As a kid, I probably had the same misconceptions about magic as everybody else, but when I started digging, I realized that its really a technology; it's a series of procedures and people don't normally associate scientific method with magic. The great Egyptian magicians were also temple priests, so religion and magic all came out of the same buildings. Some of these temples still have formula written on the walls; A couple of magicians who lived in the 2nd Century A.D. were writing down what it was that they did and what the results were, and this has been tested so many times and it works."

"I had to learn classical Greek to be able to read these papyri and I went through every single papyri known connected with magic. I went through every single spell and worked out what the methods were," he tells The Higherside Chats show. "In the Sorcerers or magicians' manuals dating from the 1200's, I found remarkable similarities, in that the techniques were very similar, even though the names of the spirits that were called would quite often be different. Then I moved to Asia and met up with Chinese magicians, and what they did.

I was gobsmacked to discover, that the techniques again were the same, so I think we are talking about something quite real here because if they weren't the same, you know, if people just made up gibberish every time, but these techniques were all parallel – so, looking at magic from a scientific perspective, I think that is most interesting.'

'20th Century magic has sort of become a question of visualizing and doing mental exercises and things – but Spells are nothing to do with mental exercises – it is a specific formula and it is to do with independent Spirits, Angels, whatever you like to call them and real magic consists of calling these entities, constraining them, binding them and getting them to do what you ask them to do.

They can't do everything – it's not like in a children's storybook; there are very specific things they can do and in fact, specific spirits have specific specialities and if you ask them to do something that's not , as it were, on their list, then they just plain can't do it; but if you call the correct entity and you call him at the correct time of day and you do the procedure in the correct way and you ask him to do something, or you tell him, or you order him to do something, then 9 times out of 10, that thing will happen.

There is this sort of direct line transmission of spells from the Greek – Egyptian magicians, which then became the source of the Key of Solomon. I was lucky to have had a good physical manifestation in my late teens as a result of working with a Grecian magic and I managed to bind that spirit, and so from then on, I had the help of that spirit to bind other spirits."

But he warns; "You need protection from the spirits. Those people who attempt to call spirits without any protection are really playing with fire. It is common to consecrate a circle on the floor around the operator and then to place a spirit loci or triangle into which the spirit need to be forced to manifest – if that's not done, the spirit will either not come or will come and lie and will not do what you tell it to do."

It would appear then, from this expert scholar, that the

conjuring and binding of spirits to do your bidding is very real. If you call them in the right way, which Skinner has decrypted and decoded from the ancient Greco-Egyptian texts, then making disembodied entities come into our world to do our bidding, good or evil, they will do it, and this could mean death to your enemies if you so choose. Or, is this just fanciful thinking? – Well, dabble with casting spells and curses at your peril!

One wonders, where is this mysterious woman who cast a Spell upon Christopher Case now? And has she claimed any more victims?

Chapter Four:

'The Cunning Man.'

It's a strange tale of a murder that has all the elements of a rural community ensconced in ghosts, witchcraft, ancient beliefs and ritual practises that could even entail the sacrificing of a human in exchange for favours from the gods of the underworld.

The victim, Charles Walton, born 12th May 1870, was killed on Valentine's Day, February 14th, in 1945, at his farm called The Firs, which sits on the slopes of Meon Hill, Gloucestershire England, a location that is also known as the place Tolkien had in mind when he wrote of Weathertop in the Lord of the Rings, but it's also known more infamously for an incident in the 1940's simply referred to as 'the witchcraft murder.' Amid this quiet rural landscape, a local famer called Charles Walton was killed with his own pitchfork, and into his chest was carved a cross.

At the time of the grisly murder, he was 74 years old and he had resided there in the area of Lower Quinton for his whole life. He had been married but was a widower now, although he did not live alone. He shared his small cottage with his 33-year-old niece Edith Isabel Walton, who he had adopted when her mother died many years ago. Other than that, he was known to be a bit of a solitary figure who seemed to prefer his own company, according to those who lived nearby, although he was not disliked necessarily but as we shall discover, there were mixed feelings about him.

He'd been a farm labourer for many years, but as a young man he had gained the reputation for being a skilled horse trainer. On the day of his strange murder, he'd left his cottage carrying his pitchfork and a hook used for pruning – this was a sharp double-edged implement with one sharp side and one concave side for cutting. Two people saw him walk through the graveyard, sometime between 9 and 9.30 am. He was walking with a stick although carrying his farming implements. The stick he needed because he now suffered from arthritis in his joints. He still worked though, as he had to, as everyone did in the agricultural community he lived in, to pay for his food and other necessities.

For the last few months, he had been hired as a farm labourer by the local farmer Alfred Potter, at his farm The Firs. Walton's task that day was to trim and prune the hedges in a field called Hillground, on Meon Hill. World War II was ongoing at this time and his niece meanwhile worked as a Printer's assistant at the Royal Society of Arts, who had moved their offices to Lower Quinton because of the War.

As Walton set about his task of pruning the hedges in the field, the day passed uneventfully, or so it would seem. He would usually return home to his cottage around 4 pm, according to his niece. She would return later, at around 6 pm. When she returned that evening however, her reclusive uncle was not in the Cottage. He was not one to drink in the local pub in the evenings and he was not in the habit of visiting friends. He was not only a solitary character, but he was also a creature of habit and so for him not to be home in the evening was highly unusual and hence it was an immediate concern for her.

Edith left the cottage and called upon her neighbour, a farm worker called Harry Bearsley. He had not seen her uncle either, and so together they decided to walk to the farm her uncle was employed at. When they arrived, farm owner Alfred Potter told them he'd last seen Walton earlier that day in Hillground field trimming hedges.

The three of them set off toward Hilldown, arriving at the spot in the field where Potter had last seen him. As they searched the area, they were shocked to discover the body of her uncle, lying on the ground near the hedgerow. He appeared to be lifeless. His neck had been slashed, most likely with the sharp blade of his own pruning hook, and the prongs of his pitchfork had been driven into his neck, pinning him to the ground with it. The handle of the pitchfork had been wedged under the hedge. The hook was still buried in his neck. The pitchfork had been thrust so violently into Mr. Walton that the two sharp prongs had been bent backwards. His walking stick was found nearby covered with blood and some of his hair was attached to it, indicative of a violent beating. Cut into his chest was the shape of a cross.

The scene was so gruesome that Edith went into shock and started screaming. What those who found him most remembered was the look of sheer horror in the dead man's eyes. At his autopsy however, Professor Webster's post-mortem, while indeed finding grave injuries to Walton's neck, with his trachea cut, and severe injuries to his chest too, including several broken ribs, his autopsy report makes no specific mention of the cross said to have been carved into his chest. Had it been? Was it left out to keep it quiet? – so as not to alarm people, because of its ritualistic and satanic undertones?

While Edith was screaming at the sight of her uncle's brutilised body and the terror still showing in his eyes, a man named Harry Peachey happened to be passing by on the other side of the hedge and on seeing him, the farm owner Potter called out to him and showed him the terrible sight of Walton's dead and bloodied body, pinned to the ground by the hook and pitchfork. He told Peachey he must go immediately to fetch a policeman, while Potter announced that he would stand guard over Walton's body until the police arrived. Beardsley, Walton's neighbour, escorted Edith away from the horrifying sight of her uncle, leading her back down the hill.

At just after 7 pm, Policeman Michael Jones Lomansey arrived at the murder scene. Later that evening CID police arrived from the larger town of Stratford Upon Avon. Half an hour before midnight, Professor James M. Webster of the West Midlands forensic laboratory arrived and at 1.30 the following morning, Walton's body was removed from the field. Dr Webster later stated that he believed Walton had been murdered between 1 – 2pm that afternoon. His watch was missing.

Detective Inspector Tombs took a statement from farm owner Alfred Potter, who said that he had known Mr Walton for approximately 5 years since moving to the farm. He said Walton had been working for him for a period of 9 months and worked every day when the weather was fine, and that he had been working on the hedges in all of his fields over the last few months. The farm owner said that he had been in the local pub, the College Arms, with Joseph Stanley, a farmer from a nearby farm, until Midday.

After he left the pub, he said he went straight over to a small field that adjoined Hillground field and he spotted Walton working in the field then. He said from the position that Walton was in, he had by then trimmed about 6-10 yards of hedge, and when he found Walton's body later that evening, he had moved position to about half-way so that he would have had about four to eight yards left to trim. The farmer said that he knew Walton would usually stop working at around 11 am for an early lunch, and then work up until 4 pm when he finished for the day. The farmer described his employee as "an inoffensive type of man but one who would speak his mind if necessary."

A message was sent from the Chief Constable of the

county to Scotland Yard, in London, asking for their assistance in what he termed 'a brutal case of murder.' The Chief Constable said, 'The murder was either committed by a madman or one of the Italian prisoners who are in a camp nearby.' (They were Prisoners of War.) A detailed description of the missing man's watch was also circulated to all pawn shops and jewellers.

Two days after his murder, Chief Inspector Robert Fabian from Scotland Yard arrived, along with his colleague Detective Sergeant Albert Webb. They were joined by Detective Saunders of Special Branch in London, who could act as translator as he was fluent in Italian. Inspector Fabian was later memorialized in one of TV's first Police Serializations which was based on crimes during his time serving as a police inspector.

Farm owner Potter was quick to tell the police that his fingerprints would be found on the murder weapons – he had tried to pull out the hook from Mr. Walton's neck, he said, and this was watched by the two witnesses with him. While the police questioned him, and he was muddled at times in his testimony of that day, the police did rule him out as being the murderer eventually.

Initially, they had a policeman stay with him and his wife at the farmhouse, observing them, and one strange thing that he noted was the glee with which they celebrated that an Italian man was being questioned over the murder, implying of course that Potter was glad the murder was being pinned on someone other than him.

Potter's trousers that he had worn on the day of the murder, had been cleaned thoroughly by the time the police seized them. It appeared to look like there could be bloodstains on them – there were marks, but they could not be analysed. However, the police would go on to rule out both him and any of the Italian occupants of the internment camp.

The police found the investigation extremely difficult and frustrating. None of the villagers would help the police. They would not talk to Inspector Fabian. Most of them shut the door in his face when he went house to house to make his inquiries. This added to his already growing unease about the place.

On Inspector Fabian's arrival, he was told of a strange incident that had happened seventy years earlier just 15 miles away, that bore striking similarities to Mr Walton's murder. 79-year-old Ann Tennant, living in the village of Long Compton, had also been killed with a pitchfork – because her murderer, Mr James Heywood, believed she was a witch. Many of the historical accounts say that she too was slashed across the throat with a bill-hook and pinned to the ground with a pitchfork.

Fabian began to look more deeply into the history of not only Charles Walton, but the area around Lower Quinton as a whole. He was soon stunned to discover the similarities between the murders of Walton and Anne Tenant. Added to this strange fact, was the book handed to Inspector Fabian by Detective Superintendent Alex Spooner, Head of Criminal Investigations Department for the county of Warwickshire. The book was written in 1929 by a reverend James Harvey Bloom, Rector of Whitchurch. It was called 'Folklore, Old Customs and Superstitions,' and in the book was a true story about the murder victim, Mr. Walton.

The story described a true account of an incident that had happened to Walton when he was a young man. On his way home from working in the fields one day, an apparition of a large black dog stalked him. It was a huge black dog, but it was ephemeral, not real, but spectral. He said that the phantom dog appeared for several nights in a row as he walked home from the fields, and the last time he saw it, it was accompanied by a headless woman. Later that night, Mr Walton's sister died.

It was claimed that soon after Mr. Walton's own murder, a black dog was found hanging from a tree not far from the murder scene. Nobody claimed ownership of the dog. Then, Inspector Fabian himself was stalked by a huge black dog while walking at twilight on Meon Hill. The dog ran past him, and a short while later Fabian met a young boy who lived in the village.

Fabian asked him if that was his dog, to which the boy enquired, what dog? When Fabian described it, the boy apparently turned deathly white, and ran away. The black dog, you see, was thought to be a harbinger of death. Anyone who encountered it was at risk of winding up dead, or their close relations would.

"That afternoon," Fabian writes, "a police car ran over a dog. Next day another heifer died in a ditch. And when Albert Webb and I walked into the village pub that evening, silence fell like a physical blow. Cottage doors were shut in our faces, and even the most innocent witnesses seemed unable to meet our eyes. Some became ill after we spoke to them. The natives of Quinton are of a secretive disposition and they do not take easily to strangers."

In years to come, Inspector Fabian would write a book about some of the cases he worked on while at Scotland Yard, and in the book, he references 'The Pitchfork Murder' of Charles Walton. He writes, 'One of my most memorable murder cases was at the village of Lower Quinton, near the stone Druid circle of the Whispering Knights. There a man had been killed by a reproduction of a Druidical ceremony on St Valentine's Eve....I advise anybody who is tempted at any time to venture into Black Magic, witchcraft, Shamanism – call it what you will – to remember Charles Walton and to think of his death, which was clearly the ghastly climax of a pagan rite. There is no stronger argument for keeping as far away as possible from the villains. It is prudence on which your future peace of mind and even your life could depend.'

He believed Mr. Walton had been the victim of ritual human sacrifice. Like the terribly chilling movie 'The Wicker Man.' Mr. Walton, Inspector Fabian believed, had been sacrificed as an offering to the ancient druid gods. Why would Inspector Fabian believe this? Well, Mr. Walton was murdered during Candlemas. In ancient times, February 14th, the day of his murder, was the day of Candlemas in the Pagan Calendar. Candlemas is more commonly celebrated on the 1st to 2nd now, and in Fabian's time too, but he believed it could hark back to the time when it was celebrated on February 14th, centuries ago.

Candlemas is also known as Imbolc. Imbolc is the fire festival between Yule and the vernal equinox. It marks the middle of Winter and looks forward to the promise of Spring to come. It is the time of Sabbat or the Witches Festival, and the first of eight supposed annual Satanic Sabbats, each of which is said to require human sacrifice.

Mr Walton had been killed near the ancient druid stone circle called 'The Whispering Knights,' Druids being the highest level of the Pagan faith. Although it can be hotly disagreed that real human sacrifices happen; that this is just sinister slander of those who practice paganism and Druid worship; cases do sometimes crop up in the media suggesting human sacrifice can happen. Online, many 'ritual abuse' websites list a set of dates in the calendar which require the practise of human sacrifice.

And yet, if this was something that happened in the Charles Walton case, as Inspector Fabian said, why would it have been done on 14th rather than 1-2nd February? Almost all references available cite the dates of 1st and 2nd as being Imbolc rather than the 14th.

Could the perpetrators have been adhering to the most ancient date-line, to offer the purest sacrifice? In fact, February 14th is also recognised as the time of 'Disting,' according to 'The truth about Teutonic Magic' by esoteric publishers Llewellyn. In Teutonic Magic, 'It heralds the beginning of the vital forces that turned inward at the time of Winter night, and it is the time when many local assemblies are held,' so it would seem February 14th Valentine's Day can indeed be a day for ritual magic and gatherings, and witchcraft.

Regardless, at the time of Charles Walton's murder it was believed that his murder date had special significance to the Druids who had once lived and worshipped at the Rollright Stones, near where Walton's body had been found. The Rollright Stones and 'The Whispering Knights' are a collection of ancient standing stones like Stonehenge and an ancient burial chamber.

The Whispering Knights predate the Rollright Stones by possibly more than 1000 years and it is a 'portal dolmen' burial chamber. The Whispering Knights dolmen is one of the most ancient portal tombs of

Neolithic Britain, built around 3,800 B.C. 'Dolmens' are Portal Tombs, and they mark burial places in a very distinctive way, with large capstones elevated at an angle and held up by huge standing stones. It is a burial chamber that consists of four upright stones and a large fallen capstone. It is estimated that using rollers and levers it took up to 60 people to move the stones.

The legend of the stones is that the king and his knights were outwitted by a witch there. The witch turned them all to stone then turned herself into an elder tree to watch guard over them. Centuries ago, a local farmer once supposedly took one of the stones to make a bridge over a stream. It took 24 horses to drag the stone down the hill and a man was killed on the way. When the capstone was placed across the stream, unearthly noises began to be heard and the farmer soon returned the stone to its rightful place.

'Some without being told of the reputation of the circle even have nightmares where they enter a cave beneath the circle and see a young woman transformed into a snake,' writes Steve Evans. 'It was well known even as early as Tudor times that the Rollright Stones, or 'Roilig' meaning Church of the Druid, were a meeting place of witches.'

According to the Folklore Journal of 1895, Dr A. J. Evans reported that one William Hughes of Long Compton had seen the fairies many times as had his mother too. In the late 19th century, Will Hughes, from the village of Long Compton had once seen fairies dancing around the King Stone. His widow Betsey's mother, had apparently been 'murdered as a witch.' It is said that underneath the King Stone fairies live. They emerge from them at night.

In 1662, a woman named Isobel Gowdie was burned as a witch. Her neighbours had suspected the old woman of using teams of toads to plough the fields near her home. Most likely because of his ability as a youth to train horses, Charles Walton gained the reputation not only of being a 'horse whisperer' but of having dominion over all animals, having power over birds, and of breeding giant natterjack toads who would do his bidding.

It was feared among the locals that Charles Walton was a powerful witch. In Walton's case, the locals believed he harnessed his giant toads to a miniature plough that he kept in his garden and made them act out the ruining of the neighbouring farmers' crops. They believed he had the ability to cast the evil eye. He was believed to have caused both the crops and the livestock to have withered. The harvest of the year before his death had been a very poor one and locals wanted to blame him. The farmer he worked for had lost a valuable heifer just the day before Walton was killed.

It was said that the only way to stop Walton ruining livelihoods was by killing him and sacrificing him to the gods to appease them and make the crops and animals flourish again, or so they were said to have believed. His blood offering in the field would be a gift back to the gods of nature and fertility. This was particularly important at this time of Imbolc, February 14th, to mark the coming season of spring and new growth.

This wouldn't be the first time a 'witch' had been

sacrificed. The area of Quinton, so close to the Whispering Knights, held a tradition of sinister happenings. In the 1870's, a widow named Anne Tenant was savagely killed by a young man who believed she too was a witch. The method in which her killer John Heywood slayed her, is remarkably similar to the killing of Charles Walton. "I pinned her to the ground with a pitchfork before slashing her throat with a bill-hook to carve a cross," he confessed. In his confession, Haywood promised he would "kill all the witches in Long Compton, and that there were sixteen of them."

The Stratford upon Avon Herald, dated 24th September 1875, reads, 'The only reason that can be assigned for the murder is that Hayward, for some time past, had been under the impression that he was influenced by witchcraft and that Mrs Tennant and several other women in Long Compton were witches, and he was determined to rid the village of them.'

Haywood had been heard blaming the witches for crop failure, and for the death of his father. He didn't kill

Tennant exactly the same way as Charles Walton actually. Upon leaving the pub quite drunk one day, he came up on her from behind and attacked her head and legs with his pitchfork. She died later that night from her injuries.

He was found guilty by reasons of insanity and sent to Broadmoor Lunatic Asylum where he remained until he died. Anne Tenant's husband John said at the trial that he had been told by her murderer that his daughter was also a witch and Heywood said he told him he "had them all in a bottle," keeping the witches as prisoners inside of it. His Doctor, George Hutchinson, said that Hayward used to come to him for medicines. The doctor said he attributed Haywood's strange behaviour to deafness and despite the killer being sent to the lunatic asylum after his trial, his doctor testified that their usual conversations were about the weather and crops and that he appeared to be sane enough on all subjects which they discussed.

Another doctor however, Dr. Parsley, examined him for the trial and found him of 'weak and feeble mind' and said that Heywood had told him of his belief in witches after having paid a visit to a "Cunning Man" named Manning at Croughton. (The Cunning folk of Britain were professional practitioners of folk magic, from the mediaeval period onwards). This 'Cunning Man' was also known as a 'Water Doctor' who specialised in diagnosing a person's ailments by peering into a jar of the person's urine. The Cunning Man said he could see a number of particles floating in Haywood's 'water,' as it was more commonly referred to, and that these particles were the witches behind the problems in his life. This diagnosis was thought to have contributed greatly to Heywood's belief that there were witches around him seeking to do him harm.

Heywood was not the only one who believed that there were at least sixteen witches in Long Compton, the village nearby to Lower Quinton where Charles Walton had been killed with the pitchfork. An old saying in the area was 'There are enough witches in Long Compton to draw a wagon-load of hay up Long Compton Hill.' The great- great granddaughter of Anne Tenant says that witchcraft was widely believed in in the area. She mentions Richard Clarke, the son of an eyewitness to the murder of Ann Tenant, who later wrote in 1928 of other instances of witchcraft in the area, including the tale of Granny Faulkner, a woman who was said to be able to transform herself into a range of animals.

On December 3rd, 1867, John Davis was sentenced by Warwickshire Assizes to 18 month's hard labour for 'wounding with intent to do grievous bodily harm.' His victim was Jane Ward. He claimed she was a witch who had sent headless ghosts down his chimney to haunt him and his family.

Going back to Charles Walton's murder now, the method used to kill him was similar to an Anglo-Saxon practice. It was called stacung, stanging or 'sticking' and involved impaling the bodies of wiccans or witches with spikes. In the 1940's the schoolmaster at Lower Quinton, A.W. Dobson, reported that the local blacksmith had shown him antique iron spikes once used to "pin down victims during black magic rites," says Michael A. Howard, writer for The Cauldron, a long-established Pagan, Wicca and Witchcraft magazine, founded in the 70's and leaning away from the more popular Gardnerian traditions of witchcraft.

He writes of witnesses reporting seeing witches dancing around the Rollright Stones near Lower Quinton. 'In 1949 on Mayday, Mr J.F. Rogers said he counted half a dozen people wearing cloaks. They danced widdershins back-to-back around the standing stone, as described in old witch trials.' 'Widdershins' is moving ant-clockwise, in a direction contrary to the sun's course, and is considered as 'unlucky,' so in other words, it would seem to be an action meant to be negative rather than positive, to cause negative repercussions and results, like black magic.

The witness 'heard mumbling and saw the leader of the group wearing, he described, a "goat-face mask," making "signs and gestures" as he stood by the King Stone.' Howard adds that in the 1950's, police were sent to patrol the stones due to the influx of ritual activity there. 'Dowser Tom Graves reported finding the mutilated body of a puppy. He described the atmosphere as "horrific."

Modern witch Lois Bourne says, 'There have been unsavoury activities at the stones on particular days in the occult calendar, resulting in special protection of the site at these times.' Says Howard, 'Witchcraft was and still is rife. In Country houses and cottages in the Cotswolds witches had their own personal shrines. In Snowshill Manor, once the home of a sugar magnate who was an alchemist, the National Trust discovered a 'magician's den.' On the floor was a magical circle and pentagram and in the room was a 'hand of glory' made from human fat.'

During the police investigation into Walton's murder, a letter was sent to police and the local newspaper by someone from Wolverhampton who said their name was "Mrs. Jones." The mysterious writer of the letter claimed that she was a witch and the former lover of the infamous occultist Aleister Crowley. She then confessed that her coven had murdered Charles Walton in a blood ritual sacrifice, but the police didn't take her letter very seriously. They thought she was probably just a fantasist and making it up. Was she?

Just a year before Walton's murder, there was a famous trial of a Witch. Medium Helen Duncan, who had been deemed a 'witch' for her uncanny ability to predict events that were not yet publicly known during World War 11. She was arrested and tried for being a Witch. She was sentenced to 9 months in prison although astonishingly, Prime Minister Winston Churchill, who was a believer in the supernatural and in spiritualism, intervened and facilitated her early release.

The village of 'Long Compton,' 20 minutes away from where Charles Walton was killed with the pitchfork, says Howard, editor of The Cauldron magazine, 'has long been renowned as a Witch Village. A young man was said to have sold his soul to the Devil in the centre of the field where the paths cross. The pact was sealed and signed in his own blood. Shortly afterwards, he caused a scandal at the Fair when he summoned a spirit in the shape of a black cockerel.'

'The oldest coven in England,' resided in Long Compton, claimed Oxford 'Cunning Man' Norman Gills.' 'Cunning Man' Gills had owned a pair of stag antlers that he said had once been ritually used by this oldest group of witches, according to Howard. 'They may have been the same group who were mentioned when the police were investigating the ritualistic murder of farm worker Charles Walton,' says Howard.

'It was said that three men and four women still lived in Long Compton and were survivors of a "witchcraft cult" that originated before 1900. Allegedly they still met on Meon Hill, a place associated with a demonic horned huntsman, hell-hounds and a black dog.' Meon Hill was where Walton was killed, and where Inspector had his run in with the supernatural black dog, as had Walton too, many years earlier.

When Charles Walton's body was found, his chain watch was missing – so at first the motive could have been a robbery, albeit that his killing was carried out in a very bloody way, but rather than witchcraft. An Italian from the Internment camp nearby was questioned as a likely suspect – however, the watch would not have been worth much money, and in fact the Italian man, who had been found with blood-stained clothes, confessed not to murder but to illegal poaching, and was cleared of involvement.

It was also later revealed that in fact inside the watch case, Walton carried not a watch at all but rather, a piece of highly polished black glass, which was believed to be used as protection against witches, or to cast spells, and that it was this that the witches had been after, not his watch, and that this was why he had been killed – to get possession of this mysterious item. The mystery deepened in 1960, when his missing watch was found in an outhouse by a worker who was demolishing it behind Walton's cottage. Nobody could figure out how it had got there.

In 1950, with the crime still unsolved, Professor Margaret Murray, an expert in European witchcraft claimed that the murder had been the climax of some ghastly form of ritual sacrifice. "The belief is that if life is taken out of the ground, it must be replaced by a blood sacrifice." She was adamant; "Witches still exist in England. Men as well as women can be witches," explains the Professor. "A pitchfork is the symbol of a man witch. All our country districts have witches."

Walton's murder has never been solved. Interestingly, in 2015, the skeleton of a 1,400-year-old woman was uncovered by a metal detector enthusiast, close to the Rollright Stones and close to the field where Charles Walton was found impaled by the pitchfork.

The skeleton dated back to the Saxons, and it was believed that this could be the remains of a witch. She had been buried with a patera – an early Saxon religious and occult ritual utensil used to make offerings to the gods. A patera resembles a ladle and it would be filled with burning embers, and food or wine would be put into it, as an offering to the gods. This led to the suspicion by experts that the woman who had been buried was engaged in high witchcraft.

A Mr. Charles Wood, 44, made the astonishing discovery of the skeleton when he was out with friends on a social dig. When the metal detector indicated it had found something, Mr. Wood discovered the patera buried about 14 inches deep. Knowing that more may be buried there, he then left and contacted the local 'Finds' officer Ann Byard, who arrived the following day. This was when the skeleton was unearthed; of a small female who had been placed in the earth with decorated antlers buried beneath her, another pagan witchcraft item... This was why experts believed they had unearthed an ancient witch. The area it would seem, is a highly mysterious and murky one, with closely-kept secrets of the supernatural.

Chapter Five:

An Icy kiss.

On the evening of 1885, Sir George Reresby Sitwell was celebrating his 25th birthday by holding a party at his ancestral residence, Renishaw Hall in ….. Not long after the ladies of the party had retired to their beds for the night, one female guest came back out of her bedroom to tell Sitwell that she could not sleep in the room he had given her. When he inquired why that was, she explained that she had felt something cold kissing her in bed. (She was the only person staying in that room.)

Sir Sitwell found this rather amusing, however, when his friend Mr. Turnbull heard about this, he had reason to pause because Mt Turnbull explained that a few years earlier, another female guest who had slept in the same bedroom, had also asked to move rooms, after fleeing her bedroom in distress and telling all who would listen to her that she had been lying in bed asleep when she had been woken by something ice-cold kissing her on the lips.

Still Sitwell was not impressed; he's once been in the Newspapers for having debunked a séance as fake and so he was a hardened sceptic. He felt that ghosts were hallucinations or delirium especially if a lady reported seeing one.

Some years later, when renovations were being carried out on the ancestral home, workers discovered an empty coffin under the floor boards of the room both women had tried to sleep in. Who the coffin had been for, and why it was now empty and hidden under the floor boards, has never been solved.

Chapter Six:

When the Devil came to play cards.

Glamis Castle was built in the 14th Century and it is where the mother of Queen Elizabeth II grew up. It is located beside the village of Glamis in Angus, Scotland, and set in the lowland valley of Strathmore with land of more than 50 acres. It has a reputation of being extremely haunted by a number of apparitions.

The Lady of Glamis, Lady Janet Douglas, was accused of murdering her husband by poisoning him and using witchcraft to destroy the King of Scotland, King James V. She was burnt at the stake in 1537 in Edinburgh, though few believed her to be guilty of the crimes for which she was charged. She has been seen running up the stairs of the clock tower, leaving a trail of ash in her wake. Another female ghost has been seen, and this apparition has a face and mouth but no tongue. She lurks in the park surrounding the Castle.

The most notorious ghost of the Castle however is the Earl of Crawford, a nobleman who visited the Castle in the 15th Century. The story goes that one night, he got vey drunk and he demanded that someone among the other guests must play cards with him. The Sabbath was fast-approaching, and gambling was considered an inappropriate past-time for a holy day. When there were no volunteers, he declared that he would play the devil himself then.

It is said that it was not long after this declaration that a mysterious hooded man arrived at the Castle, dressed completely in black, and he offered to play the Earl at cards. One of the servants peeked through the keyhole to watch the Earl and the stranger, only to be blinded in one eye by a dazzlingly bright light.

When morning came, the Earl had vanished. Visitors to the Castle have reported hearing the roll of dice, the clinking of glasses and voices swearing loudly. When the famous novelist Sir Walter Scott stayed the night at the castle, he wrote; 'As I heard door after door shut after my conductor had retired, I began to consider myself as too far from the living and somewhat too near to the dead.'

At this Castle there is also the legend of the unknown prisoner, who was held in a hidden chamber. According to 'Notes and Queries,' 'In this secret hidden chamber was a monster who was the rightful heir to the substantial property but he was kept locked away because of his appearance – he was deformed and completely horrifying to look at – and described as 'a hairy toad – a creature too frightful to behold,' with a huge round body and tiny arms and legs.

His room was bricked up after his death, it was said. The alternative version is that in every generation of the family, a vampire child is born, and the vampire children are all bricked up in that room...

Chapter Seven:

The Headless Woman

Newspapers of January 1898 reported a mysterious figure with "the ghastly appearance of a headless woman," was haunting an isolated crossroads outside of Buckingham, England. This unpleasant apparition was witnessed first by a reputable landowner in the area and a companion, who had the unfortunate experience of encountering the phantom while out in their horse and trap.

The landowner later reported; "The night was advanced and dark." His horse began to "tremble like a leaf." In front of them, they saw a black figure standing near a post at the crossroads. The figure was blocking their path and the landowner called out to the figure, but there was no reply and it did not move. As they came closer, they noticed that the figure appeared to be a woman and the horse refused to go any further.

"What are you doing there? Move along!" the landowner said to the figure. Again, the landowner received no reply. The horse however now went into a panic and began to back-up until the trap landed in a ditch, forcing the landowner and his companion to jump out and seize its reigns before it bolted.

It was during this that the black apparition vanished. However, after the two men climbed back into the carriage, intending to leave the area at speed, the black headless figure of the woman appeared once more, standing completely motionless in the exact same position as before.

The landowner, his nerve now completely gone, asked the black motionless figure to answer him in the name of God. It was at those words that the spectral figure began to slowly move, drifting away until it appeared to float through the thick deep hedge beside where it had stood.

The landowner and his companion were quick to leave the country lane as fast as the horse would travel. They were not the only ones to encounter this jet-black headless spectre, but as word began to spread, few became willing to use that route in the dark anymore.

Chapter Eight:

Stalked

A gentleman called Clint contacted me a few months ago after hearing me on a radio show, to relate a series of very unnerving incidents in which he is stalked by something that is impossible to define; 'I was born in Granite City, Illinois, across the river from St. Louis MO. I spent most of my life in the inner city till I was 12 years old when we moved into the south central of Missouri Oxark's. For me it felt surreal, being in the country after a 12-year-old life-time in a concrete jungle.

As a child of the city, you were always afraid to walk alone at night. We carried weapons, travelled in groups for protection, had escape routes planned out where we could disappear fast in miles and miles of what seemed to me to be endless humanity. Then, at 12 years old, that all changed. I felt safe walking old country roads at night. Houses could be 2 or 3 miles apart instead of cramped and packed in together. You could walk all night and never see anyone. At School my older brother and I made friends with some neighbours about three miles from us. My older brother was more friendly with Bruce, who was more his age, and I made friends with Paul, he being more my age.

One Saturday, I got bored and decided to walk to my friend's house, which I didn't do much cause it was a long walk, but off I went, and when I get there my older brother is already there talking to Bruce who is obviously still in a state of shock and fear by the look on his face. He told us; "Something followed me last night while I was walking home. I thought it was a squirrel at first, then it came closer, got heavier, like a cow, then even closer and heavier. It kept pace with me through the woods till I came to a field and I thought I'd die when it would show itself but, there was nothing to see.

It's still next to me only 10-20 feet away but, there's nothing to see and this thing must be as big as an Elephant by now." I remember thinking OMG I hope that never happens to me, and the look of fear on

Bruce's face haunted me anytime I walked dark country roads after that.

In time however I forgot about it, walking county roads at night (when I had to) was peaceful, relaxing. I enjoyed the solitude. Then, one night, fifteen years later in 1985, when I'm 27 years old, it happened to me. I had an old beat-up pick-up truck that I only used for short trips because it had a tendency to fail me on occasion and I'd have to leave it on the side of the road till the next day when it would decide it would serve me once again and start back up and run just fine.

About three miles from my house was an all-night truck stop called the Oasis which had gotten honourable mention in the Garth Brooks song "Friends in Low Places" and I had gone there to meet a friend that never showed, so, I left there about 3 a.m. About half a mile from there my old truck once again failed me. No big deal, I'm only three miles from home, so I leave it where it stalled and start walking.

It was one of those nights when the moonshine is so

bright you can see your own shadow and can see for miles. About five minutes after I start walking it started. Quiet at first, it starts deep in a thick of woods and its keeping pace with me, which unnerves me. During the day it would have been hard to keep pace in the tangle of woods, but, at night would be impossible, it made me aware that this was unnatural, whatever this was whether squirrel or deer, should not be able to keep pace with me like this at night.

It very quickly started coming closer through the woods and I became aware that this (thing) was bipedal, walking on two feet, as it came closer. I move to the other side of the road and keep my eyes on the woods as I walk.

Up ahead around a bend in the road is a field that someone had bulldozed a section of woods into a deep hollow at the far end of the field. As I come to this clearing I tell myself that whatever this is will be plain to see in the moonlight once it's out of the wood's and it'll be something I should have known or expected would be there and I'd feel silly that I, a grown man, had been afraid in the first place. But, from the sounds it made in the woods, I knew that was not going to happen.

Situations like this make a person cast about for a reason. You tell yourself that it's anything except what you can see or hear (or not see). However, when I did come to the clearing it got worse. It came closer, was louder, from the sound it made; It must be a couple ton's. I'd heard cattle run before, and they make a heavy sound from their weight, but this was much heavier, and like I've said, bipedal.

Now it's out in the open and I still can't see whatever this is. I'm on the far side of the road and this is from what I can hear no more then thirty feet away, just on the other side of the fence and I should be able to see something, but, there's just this LOUD thumping sound it makes as it walks next to me. If I walk faster, it walks faster, if I slow, it slows, if I stop, it stops. I then remember back all those years ago of the look of fear on my friend Bruce's face and how I'd felt dread that such a thing should ever happen to me, and now I'm thinking, this is real, this is happening.

By now the fear is so palpable. If I'd had a knife I could have cut you off a piece and handed it to you, but, in spite of instinct to run, I keep a façade of calm and just walk, running would give whatever this was reason to give chase. I keep walking by force of will and keep my eyes on the field next to me and my sights on the brush pile at the end of the half-mile long field, there are whole trees in that pile and it's twice as high as my house; whatever this was had to stop once I got there.

But, it didn't. It just kept on going straight through the brush pile tearing up country as it did. Now, I could try and explain the sound of a five-ton spook tearing through brush but there's just no way to describe it. POW, POP, SNAP. Still not good enough. But, I will tell you this, once and once only. I screamed, like a school girl and took off running. I've never done that before you know, screamed in fear I mean.

It stands to reason that it must have stopped following me, I mean, I'm still here, but, I don't remember the run the rest of the way home. I don't think I was abducted or anything like that, my opinion is that I was fear blanked. This is no-where near the end of this story. I've talked to several people with similar stories of what I think is this same creature that I now call stick man.

A couple months after my encounter I was talking to my brother and told him what had happened and half expected him to call bull..., cause that's how he is, one of those people that doesn't believe in anything. Anyway, he told me that around the same time (different night) he and his friend Steve were sitting on the hood of their car down by the Gasgonade river which is just outside our town and near where I'd had my scare, when they started to notice that they were hearing a noise across the river on the other side of a field that was next to the one were I'd had my scare.

He said it started up top of a wooded hill about a half mile from where they sat. It was loud enough that they could hear it from that distance as it came down the hill and into an open field and continued toward them, getting louder all the way the whole time and, as with me, there's nothing to see, and, like me, they can't get their heads around that fact.

"We can't see anything," he told me, and from the sound of it there should be a house walking toward them. It finally crossed the field and came to the line of brush that grew along the river and tore through the brush to the river and jumped in and started toward them and the whole time, there's nothing to see even though he and his friend could see the splash it made as it swam toward them.

While he was telling me this story, he told me he had an overpowering urge to get in the car and beat it outta there long before it made it halfway across the field, but, being young and all that, he wasn't going to be the first to turn tail and run, not with his friend there. It was when it jumped in the water and started swimming toward them that they both lost their nerve, jumped into the car and fish tailed it outta there.

Now comes the story of Jack. Jack was a tattooed hippie type that once told me during a conversation about whatever this was that had followed me and scared my brother that he (Jack) welcomed the unknown no matter how dark. Yeah, he was a little on the scary side.

We were having these conversations every morning because I was Jack's ride to work and every morning he would walk to my house have coffee and kill time till it was time to leave for work. He lived about a mile from me outside of town and sometime during the first week he started riding with me to work he just sort of mentioned in an off-hand don't care kinda way tells me: "Something followed me in the woods this morning; it does every morning."

When I ask about it he tells me basically the same story that my brother and I shared. He told me it started the first day he started walking to my house to catch a ride to work. "If I'm walking next to the field, it's in the woods. If I walk next to the wood's, it's in the field," he told me. He said it was there every morning. When I ask if he could see it, he said he thought it was hiding from him because he was trying to get a look at it.

He told me; "When it's on the other side of the road in the wood's I try and surprise it and jump to the other side of the road and it appears to go into the field. Then I jump to the other side where the field is and it goes back into the wood's." It went like that for a couple months, then one morning he comes in for coffee and tells me; "I saw it. It was in the woods and when I jumped to the side of the road where it was this morning, it didn't go to the other side into the field this time. It was behind a tree and it moved so fast that it was a blur but it would stop long enough for me to get a good look at it."

Jack told me it was 8-9 feet tall and was black and looked like a stick man, the kind of stick figure we used to draw as children in school. He said it moved so fast that it wavered into a blur as it moved back and forth between trees and that's what made the sound of loud walking that my brother and I had heard, then it would stop so he could see it, standing still for a few seconds, then start the blurry wavy movement again.

Since then my friends and I just call it stick man. This all happened a long time ago. I don't walk county roads much these days but every once in awhile I hear someone brag that they're not scared of anything and that they're gonna go out in the woods and dare any kinda bogie to show itself. My advice is, don't go, you'll find what you're looking for......'

In April 2013, John wrote an account of a very strange experience he'd had the night before. He had gone on the internet to try to find an explanation as to what it was that he had seen. He found people who had also sent in their strange encounters, and he described his, hoping someone else would recognise his experience and be able to make sense of his. He says; "I live in Northern Minnesota in a small town. I was out walking my dog on our usual route at around 9.15 pm. Out on the edge of town we usually walk over the bridge across the river and then come back over and head home. To get there we turn at an intersection with some street lights behind us.

As we're approaching the intersection, a tall silhouette figure walked very fast across it, dressed all in black and wearing what looked like a duster coat. With the lights behind me I should have been able to make out the person's face, but it was like he was a silhouette. There was no detail at all.

It seemed to be male, but it was moving unnaturally fast toward the bridge. My dog started to get very agitated. As I looked up again, the figure had reached the bridge, and it seemed to turn and look at us, but I can't be sure. How fast it had reached the bridge and yet it had made no sound. It's a quiet spot – I should have heard footsteps.

I was very aware it was "aware" of us. I kept telling myself this was all in my mind and yet as I was walking closer, my alarm bells were going off. I've been training in martial arts for the past thirty or so years; I also teach students defence tactics; but my training has taught me if it feels wrong, it is. I turned 180 and started walking away. I swear I could feel it's stare on my back as I walked away. It was so intense that I couldn't help but look back around to make sure it wasn't moving up behind me…. I have to admit I am still uneasy about this situation….'

Chapter Nine:

The 'Fighting Ghost of Tondu'.

In 1904, reports came from the Welsh village of Tondu in Bridgend County, that they had acquired a sinister inhabitant. The reports reached as far as Australia, as Newspapers regaled its readership with the exciting details. 'A Ghostly Reign of Terror in Glamorganshire,' exclaimed the headline of the South Wales Echo. For some time, there had been talk of the disused colliery being haunted. Then, on an early September morning, workmen saw a tall spectre shrouded in white, in the neighbourhood of Felinfach.

The 'ghost' glided towards them with a drawn-out "Booh!" The spectre's great black sockets where its eyes should have been, were fixed straight ahead, and all twelve sturdy Welsh miners took to their heels and fled. When they finally dared to look back, the ghost had disappeared.

Extremely combative, this ghost reportedly put twelve strong men to flight, and wrestled another. A servant girl reported seeing 'the Fighting Ghost' stalking the ruins of the abandoned colliery, uttering 'dismal groans and waving its arms about.'

In November 1904, the West Gippsland Gazette reported on the return of 'The ghost of Tondu,' in Glamorganshire. 'It has reasserted itself in the most aggressive manner. A respectable resident of the district was proceeding at midnight along a lonely, narrow road adjoining the deserted buildings of the abandoned colliery, when he was attacked by the unnatural monster.'

'The gentleman is muscular, but the sight which suddenly met his gaze at the far end of a bridge made him turn hot and cold. An exceptionally tall, cadaverous figure was standing there. A silent, motionless sentinel. The head, as the frightened observer describes it, was "like a death's-head covered with wrinkled parchment. The eyes were hollow sockets."

'Suddenly the thing advanced towards the trembling man. It approached toward him with long arms outstretched. It clasped him in a vice and then began an uncanny tussle in the darkness. The resident felt himself held as though in the folds of a python. He tried to flee but could not escape from the power of this supernatural assailant - then it was - gone.'

The women and children of Tondu were kept indoors after darkness fell, and bands of brave men who armed themselves with pitchforks and bludgeons of many types, took to patrolling the dark country roads by night to attempt to slay the violent Ghost. It would appear that at some point after this, no slaying actually took place but somehow the Fighting Ghost of Tondu vanished. Perhaps it was simply an answer of relocation...

'The Ghost of Golden Gate Park.'

On January 6th, 1908, the front-page story of the San Francisco Chronicle declared that a terrified group in a car were stopped by police for driving at great speed through the Golden Gate Park. After being apprehended by police on horses, the newspaper writes;

'When asking the driver why he had been driving so fast, police were shocked to discover that the group inside of the car; Arthur Pigeon and the rest comprising of a group of females, looked terribly white, as if they'd seen a ghost; which indeed they then explained they had.

'Park ghost holds up automobile party. Police are asked to run down spook who terrorized motorists. Women shriek in fright, confident that spectral visitor tried to block their progress.'

The terrified group told the officer they'd seen a "thing" in front of their vehicle, which was extending its arms as though to stop them; and "it was clad in a luminous white robe," Mr Pigeon told the officer. "It was a tall, thin figure. It was barefoot and had long fair hair. It seemed to shine. I did not notice the face – I was too frightened!"

The officer listened to the account, most bemused, and suggested that the group show him where this figure was. At this suggestion, the females in the party "shrieked," and refused to budge. Only Arthur Pigeon was capable of walking with the police officer back to the spot where he claimed he had seen the spectre.

It was no longer there; there was now no sign of it. The San Francisco Chronicle wrote that the police officer gave his report of the incident to Captain Gleeson when he returned to the Park Station later that night. Captain Gleeson then 'Gave orders that "any ghost answering this description is to be arrested on sight!"

Chapter Ten:

Something in the Woods

Country Life Magazine received a hand-written letter in February 1942, from a lady who had gone with her husband on a holiday to Scotland the previous year. She wanted to share their strange experience with the readers. 'While walking through an ancient forest, we took a short-cut through a wild glen. We came to an open space which was treeless. As we entered it, my husband remarked; "I don't like this place. It's too old and dead."

'I was about to reply that I felt it peaceful, but I suddenly had the sensation of depression amounting almost to hopelessness; what I 'saw' was more a feeling as if all about me was snow under a leaden sky, and behind me were people and their eyes were without hope. My husband saw that I was oddly frightened and so we left.

Back at the hotel, we told them we'd felt spooky at this one place in the forest. The owner, Mr Stewart said, "Ah, yes, that would be where a whole village were lost in the snow and they all starved to death.'

Neither of us are in the least psychic; but I do know that even if I were chased by Hitler and his gang (this took place during WWII) I would not enter that forest again.'

~~~~

Recently I corresponded with a man called Jeffrey. 'I'm from Parkersburg West Virginia, I hunt, fish, shoot and spend a lot of time outdoors. I really don't believe any of this - but last week something happened that I can't explain. On my way hunting at 6.30 am, driving on lost pavement road, something crossed the road in front of me, had to be at least 15ft. tall and was a medium dark brown in colour. It glided across the road just off the ground."

"When I say crossed, I don't mean walked - it kind of

glided quickly as if hovering just off the ground. It was very tall, brown and flew across the road so quickly that I really didn't see detail. All I know is, I have no idea what that was and have never seen anything like it. It was shifting rectangle in shape is best I can describe. I still can't even think what that was and I practically live in the woods."

For those who have read any of my other books, you will have come across sightings and encounters of what seem to be shimmering, almost transluscent 'entities' for want of a better word and the people have had the misfortune to run into them. We do not know what they are, but they generate a terrible sense of diquiet and fear.

Jeffrey has been a hunter all his life. He is very used to going out into the woods alone, at any hour day or night. He said, "When it happened my first and only thought was "what the hell was that" and I still can't rationalize it."

I asked him, did it have any substance to it or could you

see right through it? "Yes, it was a shifting dark brown shape that hovered quickly across the road. If you have ever seen a flock of birds tightly grouped together it moved like that. You could not see through it. It had a shape and I don't think my mind even accepted what I saw. It scared the hell out of me then. I thought that couldn't be real and tried to dismiss it. Does that make any sense?"

"Yes, it does, though what it was I do not know. But I have found other people who have had similar experiences. Almost as though something was shifting in density." I asked him, "Was there any possible shape to it at all, in terms of any formation of a head or limbs or was it completely blurred?"

"I was expecting to see deer cross the road and when it happened, I was like; "What the hell was that? That was no deer, it wasn't birds, whatever it was it was big n fast n it scared me. I don't scare easily or even believe in this kind of thing. Like I said, it happened real fast. I think my mind kind of went into a kind of shock and just couldn't accept what I just saw. All I know is it was a very large creature that hovered across the road was very fast. Never seen anything like it."

"I cannot explain and don't even know if I want to. My impression of it was it was evil. There is no way that was a living creature - it was too big, and it moved like nothing I ever saw, yet there it was. I don't know, like I said it scared me and my first thoughts was that it was evil. Yes, it knew I was there and was in a hurry to leave."

"It inspired instant fear and shock to the point that you just didn't want to believe what you just saw, but after it was gone that sense of fear and terror went with it. I'm not one of those people that think humans can know all of what exists. You can use my name I don't care. It happened, it was a real thing, people that know me know I'm not one to be full of it…. Good luck."

A while after talking with Jeffrey, he contacted me again. He asked me, "Did you see the short video I posted on YouTube? I didn't think about it when we last spoke but the area where I sighted this "Thing" is right next to a graveyard and a very old church. This area is very isolated."

On the video he adds, "Well, this is right where I saw that thing cross the road. Right in this corner here... this is Pleasant Hill Church established 1881 been here forever and right across is Pleasant Hill cemetery. It's pretty high here and it's pretty windy. Right down there where those pine trees are and that speed limit sign is where it crossed the road in front of me."

"It come up out of that hollow and down over to the right there its real deep back in there and there's a pond down in there but it crossed the road and went over near where that house and yard is and down through that field and disappeared real quick, so, I don't know what it was. Some people are trying to say it's the Mothman. We're 25 miles from Mount Pleasant where the Mothman is from. I don't know... guess we'll never know."

A commentor on it says; 'If one reads about the Salem witch trials from the people who were there it was not just a case of overzealous Christians. Some of those people were mixed up in some pretty nasty dark magic. Maybe something similar happened there at some point and let something loose.' Maybe this person has a point...

~ ~ ~ ~

Gary Macrae contacted me to explain what happened to him after hearing me talk about Jeffrey's case in a podcast interview. He writes; 'I was utterly shocked that this is going on all over, I had no idea. I have to say that this makes my own sighting even more frightening, as I can no longer brush it off as imagination, although dogs don't imagine things.'

'I can confirm that I am college educated and, until recently when I became ill, I was a software engineer for 25 plus years. I'm not mentally ill, as some may suggest, and neither is my university educated wife.'

What had happened to Gary you may wonder? Well, "I live in Kirriemuir, Scotland, which is on the edge of the

Cairngorms National Park. I read a couple of your books on holiday and was fascinated, as there seemed to be a link to several terrifying experiences I had 2-3 years ago. These were not imagination; my wife was involved also and my dogs went ballistic at the entity we saw.'

'Let me explain; around 4 years ago, I was walking my dogs at night, in the winter on a moon-lit farm track half a mile outside of Kirrimuir. I had a torch but did not have it on due to it being a clear moon-lit evening. To the left of the road, fields drop off sharply towards a small wooded area for around 200 yards. I was walking along when my dog stopped and something caught my eye.'

'I can only describe this creature/entity as something like Gollom from Lord of The Rings but almost invisible, reflecting the surroundings in the same way as the alien in the Predator films. It was taller than me, about 6-7 feet, at a guess, and it moved quickly towards the top of the hill and easily jumped a fence to end up standing crouched around 50 yards in front of me staring at me, or so it felt as I couldn't actually see the eyes. The dog was already running when I fled. I felt that it chased me but I didn't look back to find out. I ran the mile or so home, locked the doors and told my wife about it.'

'I was pretty shaken by this and we kept it to ourselves. Let's be honest it sounds pretty ridiculous. A good while passed and we had pretty much forgotten about the experiences when the most terrifying one took place. This time we were together with the two dogs, a Labrador and a Standard Poodle, which are pretty large and not easily scared, and back where I had originally sighted the entity but just on our way into the unlit area near some trees. Suddenly the dogs went apoplectic with rage and started barking like devil-dogs, looking up into a tree at the start of the farm track.'

'I shone my torch up and briefly saw the entity again, this time crouched up in the tree. The dogs were going crazy and would not go any further. We about turned and headed home. I did look back and it did not follow us into the lit area. This was terrifying as we now knew that it couldn't be imagination, as the dogs had seen it. I've never seen them so crazy before that or since that.

I could try to describe the fear but really, there are no words.'

'A few weeks passed, and we just avoided these areas at night. A few months later I was walking my Labrador in the Kirriemuir Den, which is a large un-lit park in the middle of the town. It is like a small valley with trees at the top and bushes dotted around. Again, it was a moonlit night but I was using a torch because it is very dark in there. I was walking along and had a feeling that I was being watched and the dog seemed uneasy.'

'It all came back to me and I started to sweep the torch around the hillside hoping that nothing was there, but it was running down the hill at an angle towards me, it turned away from me when I shone the CREE torch on it. The torch I use is one of those very powerful night fire models and I saw it very clearly this time.'

'It did run on two legs but also was crouched forward and touched the ground with it's very long arms as it moved. It was definitely the same thing. Around 6-7 feet tall, humanoid, but spindly like Gollum. Reflecting its surroundings. The torch shone brightly off the surface of its skin. I say skin because I don't think it was wearing anything.'

'Both myself and the dog ran like hell, out of the park and into the centre of the town. Again, although it had seen me it ran away from me when I shone the torch on it. After this I did tell a few people, I have a friend whose house backs onto this park, but nobody had heard of it or seen it.'

'Last year, we were in the woods, near where my wife saw the "predator" in a tree, and I felt that we were being followed. I also noticed that the dogs were keen to move on more quickly than usual. This time I saw nothing at all, I just had that feeling. It's like a shadow suddenly passes over your soul and you know something is wrong.'

'Being a surviving "prey" of the invisible predator myself, I can tell you that this is nothing from our world. To protect you, these entities cannot stand bright light. Shine a CREE torch at them if you are unlucky enough to come across one. If you have dogs then they are an early indicator that something is wrong. My dogs went apoplectic when they saw the "predator", it was up in a tree.'

'It is hard to spot. If you suspect something then stand deadly still and look around you. You can definitely see it if it moves, the effect is literally like the Predator film. Like a reflection on water or a distortion of light. Whatever I saw was roughly 6-7 ft. tall. It moved extremely fast; you cannot outrun it. Also, you can only see the shape, not the features. Never go out in the woods without a CREE torch of some sort, even in daylight. I hope that none of you ever see this. It is truly horrific. Terrifying."

Chapter Eleven:

The London Monster

He arrived from nowhere in the dead of night, when he came leaping out in the dark, his eyes illuminated like hot red coals, his hands resplendent with glittering razor-sharp hooks. It was 1837 in Victorian London but soon he was seen in other parts of the country, and he was most known for his seemingly supernatural ability to leap over high walls, and make boundless, endless jumps of great distances. He could scale walls effortlessly, impossibly, and vanish back into the dead of night.

He was mentioned by the Mayor of London, Sir Cowan at a private meeting, such was the growing concern over this mysterious figure. Sir Cowan read aloud a letter from a worried lady resident of London; the lady said she had heard of a wager being laid in which this trickster (a human, she believed) was being encouraged to frighten people in the following manner;

'It appears that some individuals (of, the writer believes, the highest ranks in life) have laid a wager with a mischievous and foolhardy companion, that he take upon himself the task of visiting many of the villages near London in three different disguises—a ghost, a bear, and a devil; the unmanly villain has succeeded in depriving seven ladies of their senses, two of whom are not likely to recover. The affair has now been going on for some time, and, strange to say, the papers are still silent on the subject.

At one house, the man rang the bell, and on the servant coming to open door, this worse than brute stood in no less dreadful figure than a spectre clad most perfectly. The consequence was that the poor girl immediately swooned and has never from that moment been in her senses,' says the concerned female letter writer.

So, this boundlessly leaping figure with eyes like red-hot coals and glittering razor-sharp hooks for hands, would seem to have been a 'bet' by a group of high-class pals, to dress up as a bear, a ghost or a devil, and scare the living daylights out of ordinary random citizens, and yet, if that is the case, how did 'his' eyes glow so alarmingly red, and how was he able to scale impossibly high walls and roofs, to escape? How did he leap through the air as high as a bird?

One young lady, Polly Adams, a barmaid in a pub in London, was walking home from work late one night when she was brutally attacked in Blackheath Park. She said that after being assaulted, the villain escaped by making great giant leaps. Not long after this, another young lady was attacked. Mary Stevens, a servant who worked at a wealthy home in London was assaulted on Barnes Common, another park in London. She also said that after her attacker had finished with her, he bounded away with seemingly impossible leaps.

Jane Alsop was the next victim, when she went to answer the doorbell. As she opened the door, suddenly in the dark she found a hideous monster standing on her doorstep. The figure was shrouded in a long dark cloak and stood half in the shadows. Glowing red eyes bore into hers as the figure lunged at her and she let out a scream.

This alerted her sister and father, who came running from inside the house. She later described the hideous figure as having horns and claws and it ripped at her neck and dress as she screamed in pain and terror. She, her father and her sister all confirmed that the grotesquely deformed monster then fled into the night with extraordinary leaps into the air. "His hands were icy cold," she said, but "his eyes were like balls of fire. His face was hideous. He vomited flames!" she told the police.

The police offered a reward to capture the unstoppable assailant and groups of vigilantes soon began roaming the parks and London streets, in search of the monstrous offender. The Duke of Wellington and his aristocratic friends formed their own posse, searching on horseback for the fiend, and chasing possible suspects, yet these suspects all turned out to be mere mortals and wholly innocent. Indeed, the monster was never apprehended.

As the weeks and months passed, attacks began to be reported on a regular basis; yet now the violent assaults had spread across the country. In 1855, southern England began to suffer a spate of night-time attacks. The attacker left tracks in the snow, across fields and over rooftops – routes that no mortal man could have travelled successfully without loss of life or simply couldn't have reached.

People began to call the tracks he left behind 'The footprints of the devil.' Things became so serious that the Army were called in, to capture 'the Devil.' Yet he outsmarted the Army too. They too failed to stop him. He taunted them by appearing suddenly in their foxholes, where they had hidden to stalk him.

After appearing without warning beside them in the foxhole, he would vanish again just as fast, fleeing in the blink of an eye, leaping off into the distance too fast for any soldier to catch him. Any shots fired at him were useless – he was too fast for them to hit. Before he fled however, he would slap one of the soldiers swiftly across the face with a hand that was as cold as ice. At Aldershot barracks, an hour from London, and one of the largest army bases in the country, a sentry received several ice-cold slaps to the face on night duty. Soldiers shot at the fleeting figure, but it had no effect.

In Teignmouth, Devon, down in the South-west of England, a Captain Finch was apprehended and convicted of charges of assault against two women in which he was said to have been "disguised in a skin coat, which had the appearance of bullock's hide, a skullcap, horns and a mask."

Attacks continued unabated nevertheless, long after this human foe had been jailed. Yet another report then came in from Northamptonshire, north of London, which described the attacker as "the very image of the Devil himself, with horns and eyes of flame."

There were impersonators then, such as the Army Captain; but the night-time attacks did not end. Soldiers were still slapped and ladies still found themselves confronted by the cloaked figure with its razor-sharp hooks-for-hands until gradually reports grew less and less and perhaps the monster simply relocated, or did he multiply? Did he join band with a fellow Spring Heel?

In 1877, four decades after his first appearance, Police Illustrates magazine reported on a strange incident at Aldershot Barracks. Calling the story 'The Ghosts of Aldershot;' it writes, 'A curious story comes from Aldershot. For some time, past, the sentries on two outlying posts have been frightened to death by the appearance at night of two spectral figures.

The figures, glowing with phosphorus and otherwise alarming, are in the habit of suddenly manifesting themselves, making tremendous springs of ten or twelve steps at a time, and, upsetting the wretched sentry before he has been able to collect himself sufficiently to oppose earthly arms to his ghostly visitations. The latter do him no bodily injury, contenting themselves with upsetting the poor man, after which they mysteriously disappear. So great has been the panic that it has been found necessary to post double sentries.' The legend of Spring Heeled Jack remains an unsolved enigma.

Just under a century earlier, 'The London Monster' was a big problem. First reports of 'The London Monster' appeared in 1788. This time however, it would seem he was all too human, or so it is believed. According to his victims, who were all ladies, a bulky male would follow lone women, shouting insults and obscenities at them and then stab them in the buttocks. Some reported that he appeared to have knives fastened to his knees! At least 50 women reported being attacked.

Some said he would offer them a nosegay to sniff, only for it to contain a sharp spike which he would stab their face with. Many women ended up suffering quite severe wounds as well as slashed dresses and underclothes. Women were not a little scared to venture even short distances alone, and men were infuriated that the Bow Street Runners, London's first official police force, could not catch him, although, there were only a handful of Bow Street Runners at the time.

As the attacks grew in number, a group of men, determined to put an end to it, came together to form the 'NO MONSTER CLUB,' and each wore a pin in their lapel to identify themselves as belonging to the 'NO MONSTER CLUB;' to ensure that when they were out in search of this assailant at night, they were not themselves actually accused of being him.

A young man was accused of the crime. He was a florist called Rhynwick Williams, and strangely, even though he had an alibi for many of the attacks, with the hysteria at an all-time high, he was arrested on the crime of 'Defacing clothing;' which was apparently a more heinous crime and a much harsher penalty if found guilty of than was attempted murder. The florist was sentenced to 6 years in prison. However, many historians who delved deeply into the phenomenon came to subsequently came to doubt his guilt and it's possible the real monster was never captured.

~ ~ ~ ~

In the dark and frightening days of the Nazi occupation of Czechoslovakia, a strange legend began to circulate, of a creature as frightening as the SS henchmen themselves. The horrifying phantasm was given the name of "Pérák," which translates as "the Spring Man." It was capable, according to the many witnesses, of springing from roof-top to roof-top in the dead of night under the light of the moon.

The 'Perak' liked to linger in dark alleys, preparing to launch its assaults on the unsuspecting citizens of the city of Prague. It would in wait in the shadows to jump out at factory workers returning home from their compulsory shifts working in ammunitions factories on the orders of the Germans.

Not only could it jump the roof-tops; some citizens even said they watched as it leapt over buses and speeding trains, blocks of apartments, and it would even jump the wide width of the river Vitava, the Czech national river which runs along the Bohemian Forest and then North through Prague. Reports said that it flew through the air "like a shuttlecock," before vanishing into the darkness with an inhuman shriek that sounded like a deafening shrill whistle.

At the same time as these nightly sightings, graffiti

depicting the Perak began to appear on walls all around the city. Perak became a figure of national resistance against the Nazi occupiers. People attributed the artwork to this phantom figure; yet who or what was this figure? Some citizens said the Perak was a vigilante of Czech nationality; a local person who was causing mayhem in defiance of the Gestapo regime, and indeed many later believed he was nothing more than an urban legend.

Others suggested he was an intelligence officer or a paratrooper or a spy from an allied country, who was bringing chaos and fear with the aim of scaring the workers from going to their munitions factory shifts, thus thwarting the Nazi's ability to manufacture more weapons. Whichever the case, Perak became a solid feature of Czech folklore and began to appear in comics, as Czechoslovakia's very own Superhero.

Ethnographer Dr. Milos Pulec discovered that in fact this 'legend' of a 'Springing Man' dates back much further than Prague in World War Two, tracing such legends to the 19th century when a hoax was perpetrated by

Catholic vergers in North-Western Bohemia. The Catholic Church was apparently worried about an outbreak of atheism in the local communities there, and the catholic vergers were said to have disguised themselves as "leaping devils" and leaped out at unsuspecting mining families in the region, or even deployed the use of magic lanterns which projected flying demons to scare the locals into renewing their faith in God and Catholicism out of sheer fright, according to Dr. Petr Janecek of Charles University in Prague.

He notes that often 'The Springing Man' would be confused with another supernatural figure called 'Razer Man' who, like 'Springing Man' would leap great lengths, widths and heights, but 'Razer Man' had the added horror of coming with razor blades attached to its hands. It would slash the face of unsuspecting citizens at night when it jumped out on them, and then vanished again, just like 'Springing Man' and 'Spring Heeled Jack.'

In just one of the sightings of 'Springing Man,' Miloš

Pulec quotes the memory of a boy who said; "It jumped up and after each fall, it went into a deep squat to get a proper inflection. It jumped so high it had a head almost at the height of the tram's electric power at the highest point. Every time the boots emitted a sound like throwing a brick in a deep mud. "

In another testimony, a chase was witnessed by a Josef Špiling: "In an absolutely sinister silence, the sound of the approaching train suddenly echoed, and when the first wagons began to pass, a black shadow emerged from somewhere. At that moment, the soldiers began to shoot fiercely from the machine guns. The black figure bounced off the ground, jumped over the passing train, and then, through a series of great jumps, disappeared among the trees in the darkness of the Žižkov hill."

An enemy paratrooper, a phantom, or a creature of the night?

~ ~ ~ ~

On November 10th, 1975, a Wisconsin couple had a very disturbing encounter on their front porch. A Mr. and Mrs. 'E,' of Wauwatosa, Wisconsin heard a knock on their front door that winter evening at around 7.50 pm. Mr E, who was called Peter, was 64 years old and now retired. He had formerly worked as a foreman at a local construction company, where he had worked for three decades prior to retiring. His wife Anne was 59. When the doorbell rang, she peered out of the front room window.

She saw an oddly dressed man who appeared to be holding a long white staff. She went to the front door and opened the screen door and greeted him questioningly. She asked him what he wanted, but she received no reply. She asked again but still he said nothing. That's when she called out for her husband to come to the front door.

On seeing the man for himself, her husband declared; "What's this? Something left from trick or treat?" Curiosity getting the better of him, he reached for the front door and opened it.

Later, the husband described the man in more detail. "The skin on his face was the same as smoked meat and his face was lined with deep groves." He added that the odd-looking man had just a very small pucker for a mouth, with a tiny opening only about the size of a penny, and his chin was very pointed. The 'man' was wearing a hat like a straw hat and with a narrow brim. There were tufts of hair sticking out the sides of his hat.

"Looked like an over-sized gnome!" said Peter. He really thought it was someone playing a prank on him and his wife, so he went to grab hold of the man, but when he reached his arms forward the man tapped his white staff hard on the ground and "floated backwards."

Said Peter; "He didn't step backwards or jump backwards – he just drifted away from me." Even more disconcerting and unsettling was that as Peter glanced beyond the strange man, he could see four more figures looking straight at him. Two were on his lawn and two more stood in the road. They were all looking toward him silently.

"They were all dressed alike, and they all carried this white staff in their left hands. Their feet were making walking motions, but they were two or three inches above the ground!" He added that these figures looked like they were deformed – their hands looked arthritic, all bent inwards like claws, and their legs were bowed. As they tapped their staffs down hard on the ground, they would glide and float above the ground. Peter likened it to when astronauts float in space, and when they jumped up and down on the moon landing. He believed that their staffs must wield energy to enable them to do this.

Mr. E. lost no time in running back inside his house and calling the police. At the police station, Officer Daniel Anderson, of the Wauwatosa police department had actually just received a startlingly similar phone call already about "strange people" a few streets away. The police searched for the 'men' with white staffs, but by the time they got to Peter's house, the 'men' had left and they could not be found in any of the nearby streets either.

Despite the police not really believing the elderly couple, even though they were not the only ones to report such oddly menacing men. The couples' own family too scoffed at such silliness, despite neither Peter nor his wife being in any way known as pranksters and they never changed their story.

But what puzzled Peter the most was, if it could have been explained as a prank, "The whole thing took about two minutes – why go to so much trouble for two minutes?"

And, perhaps more to the point, he asks, "And how could anyone get people to float over my lawn?" What did these 'men' want with the husband and wife? Or anyone else whose door they knocked on in the darkness?

Source: w-files.com, and http://thenightsky.org

Chapter Twelve:

"The Boys Are Coming."

Recently, I had a long correspondence with a lady called Trista, who contacted me after reading one of my other books. Her story is simply horrifying. "Nine years ago, I moved to a new house with my mother and her boyfriend. It was deep in the woods, near a quarry outside of a small town of Franktown, near Beckwith, in Ontario, Canada. A few months go by and I went into the city to meet up with my friends.

On my way back to the house, I took a cab. I let the cab drop me off at the end of the dirt road, about a 15-minute walk in the woods back to my house. Thought I'd try to save some money by walking. Bad mistake. The only light on the dirt road was one street light on a back-road intersecting with the dirt road. Fields and wooded area surrounded me, and one house.

As I was walking, it was getting darker as I moved

away from the street light. In front of me was a field of wheat. Suddenly something(s) started running in front of me. I figured it might have been deer, but after it started to circle around me on the dirt road and in the fields, I knew it was not deer. It was calculated, and it was taunting me. I ran as fast as I could in the pitch black on a dirt road to the closest house. I knocked on the door, (2am) and asked them if I could come in, something was following me.

They gave me a drive home, deeper into the woods to my house. I do believe I was going to die that night if I had not run to that house. Fast forward 3 years later. I moved into a friend's house, rented a room. I knew something was not right about the house, because every night around 3am I would hear chanting, Indian chanting perhaps?? The house was old and there was still old medicine left in the cabinets. The old lady who owned it prior had passed away.

One night I was up until 1am, laid down and all of a sudden something started telepathically speaking to me. There were at least 6 of them, but 2 of them were the nicer of the 4. The nice ones told me to run, and get out of the house quick because "The Boys" were coming.

They told me to take out the battery of my cell phone (flip phone). I asked them why, and they replied, "so they can't find you". There was 3 of them, the evil ones. I didn't believe it and thought I was going crazy until I heard the footsteps (no one else was in the house that weekend). I peeked my head outside of my bedroom in the hall and saw what looked to be a creature, who stood about 7 feet tall. Not human. I started screaming and then the creature disappeared.

I ran upstairs because that was the only way out of the house. I hid in my room-mate's bedroom in the dark, and the big bay window was shining with the street lights, and there they were. Tall, very skinny, pointy fingers, hunched, demon looking creatures. They were standing there in front of the bay window outside. They stood so still, they didn't move. I ran to my car outside, jumped in, looked back and there were the 3 figures again, this time they looked distorted, watery like? The outline was like looking through a fish bowl. In a split second, they ran at the car and the car almost tipped over from their force. They wanted me, and I'm not sure what for. I drove and never returned.'

What Trista told me got more and more disturbing; 'These "things" they talked just like humans, but they had no morals or human-like attributes, in regard to how real humans are, no conscience. These things were pure evil, taunting, threats, and mocking. There's things we can't see but are there. It really makes you think, and I think that's why we don't socialize much; because of knowing what things are out there, what is really going on behind the scenes and it's frustrating because every time I research it, it keeps leading me back to the Government. I mean none of this is good, it all stems of government, secret governments within governments which then stems out to other cults etc.'

'They looked watery... like your looking into a floating water figure, they're like there, but not. It was hard to see due to the darkness but that's what I saw again years later. You can hear them and see them for a split second or so. When there was 6 of them, one of them showed their form; it almost looked reptilian, the skin or its appearance was disfigured almost. It was so tall, terrifying. For the most part, I saw them when they looked watery, a mirage almost when they came running at the car.'

'When that night happened, I recorded everything on my netbook, in the bedroom when it took place. Strange things led up to that night, which is why I recorded myself sleeping and then eventually them or "The Boys" coming. Magically, go figure, my netbook goes missing, no-where to be found, along with a set of our house keys after I moved out that night.'

'I did consult a medium, one of the best, I heard. She turned out to be real. You're not going to believe this but 3 years ago when I did break down and needed some answers, she mentioned to me, which I didn't understand fully, still don't after I read your book about the (men's) bodies being half in and half out of the water. (Trista is referring to my book 'Dead in the water forever awake' here).

'She said to me 3 years ago when I saw her, I was half in and half out of the water. She never elaborated about that to me. I did bring it up to her about why I was there and asking about those things that came to me, and she got scared and told us to leave. After reading your book, they target men not women, in this case about the drownings, but I'm wondering if she was referring to my fiancé', and not me...'

'There is one thing I do need to mention and you can think I'm crazy or fiancé is crazy, but he is telekinesis. It was around the time that I met him/started dating that all this started happening. So I don't' know if I'm the target or if he's the target or both of us.'

'I forgot to mention, when "they" went away (6 years ago) they told/showed me how to close my mind off, they said to imagine yourself sitting in your mind, closing the doors one at a time until it's all blackness, there they said, you can be safe, you are safe in there, and then they said, "I passed." - No clue what that even meant. I do not believe the two that were "helping" me were angels, they were with the others but not as evil.'

'There's a base about 10-minute drive from my house. Strange things happen there, or rather, happen near there. Military helicopters, lights that touch the clouds coming from that direction. They claim it's a fire testing facility but, I find that hard to believe. I've seen tons of military officers heading to the building - at least 7 big trucks full of men. Anyways, everything I've seen, been through its mind boggling and really does mentally open up doors. It truly is a scary world out there into the unknown and no answers.'

'I did read near the end of your book, I think it was a professor you mentioned about the demons or such in the mind?? Spiritual attacks? I kind of related to that with my experience but still trying to figure out, why me?'

I asked Trista why she thought the "good guys" helping her were with the "bad guys" but helping her as though they had to be with the "bad guys" and had no choice.

'It's all overwhelming, and it's a mystery every day, but the first thing that popped into my head about the "beings" or "things" or simply, "they" are related to the government in some way or another,' Trista said.

She continues her story, going back to the night the "they" came for her; 'I got my boyfriend to get all my belongings and moved to a small town near where I used to live in Beckwith where the first incident took place. Carleton Place, Ontario/Mississippi Mills is where I moved, about 20 minutes from that area. 9 months later I gave birth to my daughter. We lived in a house near quarry road. One night my new-born baby and I were home alone, and my fiancé was working late at work. I cradled my child to some classical music while she slept in my arms, and then all of a sudden BOOM, something jumped down on our roof. Terrified they had come back, I ran to the phone and called my fiancé.'

'It ran to where I had ran, following me all over the house; wherever I moved, it would move, on the roof. My fiancé came home very fast. I told him what had happened, and then all of a sudden it had run across the roof again. It sounded like something VERY, VERY HEAVY. It sounded like a horse.

He ran upstairs and into the garage, to grab the cell phone, but he told me that something in his gut told him to not go out into the driveway out of the garage, because it ran to the garage where he had ran, and was waiting until he stepped out of the garage. He screamed at it to go away. Five minutes later it had left. He told me he knew he was going to die if he had left the garage.'

'The next morning, we checked the roof, and around the house for any feet prints (it was winter time and if there was someone on the roof, then we would know from the snow) there was NOTHING. No feet print, nothing on the roof, NOTHING. A month goes by and (I'm a night owl) around 2am I was reading a book with the windows open. I hear a high pitch, blood curdling scream from quarry road, in the woods.'

'It sounded like a woman was being tortured, and murdered. It made me stop breathing for a second, it went on for about 1 minute, and then stopped. It was so loud, and it sounded like it was coming from a thicket in the woods. I woke my fiancé and called the cops, the cops said they would check it out, but found nothing. They even went back the next day to the area, and found nothing. No one was missing in the area, but what if someone NOT from this area was missing?? Someone was murdered back there, and the remains were probably hidden! but no one has gone missing....'

'I'm so confused and still scared to this day. I will NEVER go into the woods, ever again. When we drive on quarry road to this day, we are always on the lookout for whoever made those screams that night. There is something stalking and hunting people that we can't see unless we really tried to. My gut tells me they feed on fear and flesh, they are always watching us, and waiting. I can still sense them watching me, waiting until I make a wrong move. I believe they can cloak and uncloak whenever they please...'

'A couple of other things has happened, I don't think I mentioned them to you, very odd stuff involving unknown men. Two men came to the door, and this may sound stupid, but it was two men dressed in black with top hats and ear pieces, they drove an expensive

Buick. We did not answer the door because of everything that has happened but my fiancé' peeked through the window and saw what they were wearing.'

'We don't have many friends or hang out or go out a lot so we know when someone is supposed to visit us, vs not supposed to visit us. Right after they left, our internet and lights went out, I think they knew we were in the house. We had a bad feeling in our gut and we left and drove for an hour after that making sure they were not following us.'

'They have not came back since. There was another man, just one man. We went to a different town to do some groceries and get some coffee. While we were at the coffee shop some strange looking man walked in with an empty black shopping bag. He never ordered anything, I'm pretty aware of my surroundings, but I caught him at the corner my eye looking at us, my fiancé and I.'

'I told my fiancé that we should head to the store and grab groceries. It was just across the street from the coffee shop. He followed us, behind us, about 20 feet, 25 feet maybe, all the way into the store. He was stalking us in the store, cookie isle, cracker isle until he directly stood right behind me pretending to look at the crackers I was looking at and listening to us. We left with a couple of things to the checkout and there he was again, at the end of the checkout isle pretending to look at the clearance items, still he had bought nothing.'

'As we walked out of the store, he walked out, but this time it looked like he was recording or had something in that black bag, he was holding it as if something was inside, pointed at us, nothing serious, but I think it was a camera or something. Fast forward 2 weeks. My fiancé and I got into an argument and he went for a walk, the same man we saw stalking us or surveillancing us drove by him in a car looking at him, and drove away.'

'I don't believe in coincidences. That man knew something, or was hired, I don't know for sure, but I have/had a gut feeling it's government. Everything always lead's back to the government some way. The more doors I opened; the more things started happening. The deeper you look into things, the more things become attracted to you. You become a beacon of light almost and it draws good and bad things to you. I've noticed it's not just spirits, but also humans. Good & bad.'

'It's hard to explain. I myself know I'm a good person, and I think things know that and try to break that down, and there are other things that protect it for me. It's hard to describe, but they are always there. It's almost like looking out of a window (the door you opened) and having a feeling that you're being "attacked" spiritually, but also protected. There cannot be a positive without a negative. There's a spiritual war going on around us, and one must be aware of their surroundings at all times in order to survive. In order to initially open those doors, one must be at their lowest point in their life.'

'It's not easy and it happened unintentionally to me, but ever since those doors been opened, they cannot be closed all the way. I've captured EVP'S on my cell phone at night, many of them, weird bird chirps in the house (we do not have a bird). I have the audio clip if you would like to hear it, of the birds chirping at 1:33am. Voices of women, voices of men, things moving in the basement, throwing things. One might deny it, but I know there are other worlds, just like this world we live in. "They" said they would be back, I just don't know when.'

'In regard to my fiancé' when I stated he could move, break things, I mean with his mind. Everything is just a little bit weird since I met my fiancé'. I know that his father's phone is tapped, with all his conversations. I also know his car break-line has been tampered with several times, which is why he sits in his chair facing the big bay window looking outside at his front door all the time. He knows stuff but cannot talk about it, Jack has told me. I don't know why they would want him dead, but he's been with CSIS, Canadian Security Intelligence Service, almost 25 years now. I just hope their attempt at harming him has nothing to do with him trying to protect us.'

'I'm always very uncomfortable going over to his house, because I can sense something, but can't put my finger on it. He does not want to babysit our daughter (5 years old), I'm not sure why, but I do know he loves her very much and is always buying her things. He uses the excuse that he's not used to kids, but I think it's just in case something happens. It's all just very confusing, trying to fit the puzzles pieces together. My fiancé can move things with his mind when he's VERY ANGRY, or when he's emotionally deep in his thoughts, even when we talk about things he's passionate about.'

'He made a song (one he remembered from his childhood) come on my laptop one night when we were talking; there was no web browser open and I don't have music on my laptop. He's also thrown books off the shelf and shattered recessed lighting before. He does not like it, he tries to avoid it and suppress it.'

I asked her; 'This might seem a strange question, but I was wondering how you met your boyfriend? (just trying to figure some of this out, and I just wondered about the background to this). Also, did the medium

give any indication why she was scared, or anything
else that she gave away? Again, this is a strange
question but do you think your boyfriend could have
been 'used' for 'mind/esoteric experiments' as a child? -
like the supposed 'Montauk boys' for example. Could he
have been used against his father's wishes /his father
forced into it/given no choice? - Or is that a bit too out-
there! sorry. Or, he was simply born with his abilities
and somehow this was picked up on by
government/military and they track him?'

Trista replied; 'These are something I ask myself
everyday. I met my fiancé' the same time those
"THINGS" came to me, so after the taxi incident. My
roommate never had anything happen to them, except
they heard a female's voice upstairs when I was
downstairs (this was before "they" came to me) I have
EVP's of a girl saying, "I haven't told them anything" on
the laptop I had that went "missing".

'I've also had sleep paralysis around that time as well,
but not anymore. I met my boyfriend online on a dating
website. He told me that when he hit his head hard

when he was around 3 years old, his skull was expose and brain matter was coming out, thankfully he survived and ever since then he's told me he can do things with his mind, as well as see things.'

'As for the Montauk project, I don't think so, but he did mention that his mother "taught" him things when he was a child, she claims to be a psychic. He only saw his father 4 times a month after his dad and mother split, but I will ask him, if he remembers anything like that. His mother taught him how to meditate and communicate with things, but he does not like to talk about it, what little he remembers.'

'He told me one night he saw a creature in the house kneeling down with yellow eyes, they locked eyes and then it ran. He said it look like a demon, but he also said it looked like it was physically there. Most people would not believe this, which is why we do not socialize with most. We like to stay in our own bubble due to the experiences we've been through.'

'The medium was scared the moment I mentioned, or

asked rather, what was on our roof that night that I mentioned to you. That's when she did a 360 and got scared. She did not want to talk about it. I do not know why. His father is mysterious, and is hiding something, I know that for a fact. I will dig a bit deeper and let you know. I do hope some of my experiences can help you in any way, or even help others, insight etc.'

Sometime later, Trista wrote again. 'I've been waiting for the right time to talk a bit more with my fiancé' about his "stuff". We just finished talking and I asked him about his cut on his head again that he got when he was around 3 years old, and I asked him if he remembers anything else and then he told me that he's been getting memories since he was a child about a farm, with a fence and a large field. He said the farm barn looked like a regular home inside, and that there was stairs in a closet going to a lower level, and there's a room that is all white, with cells holding kids.'

'He said that he's never been there before so he does not believe it, but I told him that memories like that, that you have your whole life is not normal, it means

146

something and that I think his father has something to do with it. We went into a deeper conversation and he does not want to believe but I still tried to tell him that a lot of puzzles pieces fit, especially with his large cut (scar) on his head, and his telekinesis, and (now, I just found out about it) that farm. He said he does not know where it is, but if it were to be anywhere it would be around the Smith Falls area in Ontario.'

'He says that memory only comes when he feels scared and confused, which was another red flag to me. He was almost hesitant about me involving his dad with this memory. It's very shocking to me and I'm surprised why he never brought this up to me in the past 6 years we've been together. I'm kind of in shock right now to be honest. I don't know where to start digging again.'

I asked Trista meanwhile, a little more about her boyfriend's father. And, about her mention in our earlier correspondence of cults being somehow involved.

'He works at the 'CSIS, Canadian Security Intelligence Service. My fiancé told me he does hardware but I do not know what that entails. He's not allowed to talk about it, if he does its jail, or probably an "accident". His phone is tapped as well. I do not know much about what exactly he does but I get a weird feeling from him, an uncomfortable feeling. Jack's father's dad was an escaped Nazi who fled to Jamaica. He's dead now, not sure if that is relevant or not, but figured I would mention it. Satanic cults, evil cults, groups of people who worship evil. Governments are the ring leaders and own these cults, they all trickle down eventually into cults, everything stems from top power...'

Chapter Thirteen

Disappeared by the ghost

Was an evil spirit behind a woman's disappearance? In this next story, we have the emergence of a terrifying creature of some form. In 1885, a young girl arrived to live on a rural farm in Shawville, Pontica County, Quebec, Canada. She'd been adopted by the family who lived there, farmers Mr George Dagg and his wife Susan, who lived on the farm with their children. The farm itself was located a few miles north of the Ottawa river and set amid a rich and vast forest of pine trees.

The Dagg family had emigrated from Ireland and now lived in this farmhouse, which was actually a wood cabin, comprising of three rooms. The family had two daughters, Mary aged 5, and Eliza Jane 4, and a son called Johnny who was 2. Sometimes also present was a young orphan boy called Dean who helped at the farm doing chores. The Father's parents lived a couple of miles away.

In 1885, Mr and Mrs Daggs adopted the 9-year-old girl from a placement home in nearby Belleville. Her name was Dina Burden McLean. It seemed that the young girl settled in very well with her new family, and according to all accounts she was treated very well by them and considered to be as much a part of the family as Mr and Mrs Dagg's natural children. There are certainly no reports of any problems, and it seems she wrote to her own mother to say she was happy there at the rural property.

Four years later however, the circumstances were to unexpectedly and dramatically change however, for the worse. While Mr Dagg was out working on the farm, Mrs Dagg returned home from running some errands to find a trail of excrement lining the floor of their wooden home. It seems that the mother and father, for some reason, believed this had been done by their helping hand, the young orphan boy, and he was in fact taken before a magistrate to answer for his actions. This however did not resolve the issue, after similar events happened again. Human excrement continued to be found thrown around the house. The magistrates did not find any grounds for blaming the orphan boy, but he left the farm, and never returned.

But it would seem that his removal from the Farmhouse did not stop the inexplicable events. One day, shortly after he had left, when all the family were present, one of their glass window panes suddenly violently shattered inwards. Naturally, the father believed someone was standing outside and had done this, and he ran outside to apprehend them, but he found that there was no-one there. Rather than returning back indoors, he hid outside and waited, expecting them to come back. Instead, he watched as another glass window shattered; yet there was no person there to have caused it to break.

On another occasion, one of the children was hit hard on the head when a large stone appeared to be thrown by an invisible hand, through the open door of the cabin. Then, rather more alarmingly, the arson began, but again, no human perpetrator was seen in the vicinity. Spontaneously, a total of eight separate fires broke out inside the wood cabin, causing much distress and fear and panic.

Then the personal attacks began to get more serious. Dinah, the adopted daughter seemed to be the most targeted of the family. She would suddenly experience her hair being pulled sharply. She would shriek out in pain, causing the rest of the family to run to where she was, only to find great chunks of her hair gone from her head. The same thing happened to their son too, and bizarrely most of his hair looked like it had been shorn-off his head.

One day as Dinah was helping her mother with bedroom chores, she screamed out: "Look! Look! The big black thing is pulling off the bedclothes!!"

Mary, her sister, urged her to pick up the whip and beat it and this Dinah did do – which resulted in the big black thing making a sound like a squealing pig as it vanished before their eyes. Then a mouth organ, which was lying on a shelf, suddenly raised up into the air and began playing. Then it was violently hurled across the room.

An armchair began to rock backwards and forwards, manically. A wooden moto which hung upon the wall was torn from its place and seen thumping the bed hard several times. Potatoes became the entity's weapon of choice, and each member of the family would regularly find themselves being struck hard by a flying potato.

It was not long after this that Mary saw something else just as horrifying. She saw something that appeared to her in the shape of a man but had horns on its head and cloven hooves instead of feet. It was standing silently in the doorway. Later, it reappeared to her, but this time the same figure was dressed all in white. The figure asked her; "Do you want to go to Hell with me?"

Dinah too encountered this strange 'man.' On other occasions it seemed the entity was capable of appearing to them as a huge black dog with long black hair and "tails." Local historian Greg Graham told the Ottawa Times that when this entity got angry it would slap, kick, scratch and hit Dinah.

When local people began to hear of the family's troubles, a Reverend Horner arrived to lead them in spiritual prayer. He held a group session at the cabin, and began to read aloud from the Bible, but the Bible was wrestled from his hands, and it completely vanished into thin air in front of everyone. It was later discovered inside the oven in the kitchen, but no-one in the house had put it there.

Dinah said that she started hearing a deep gruff voice talking to her. She said the voice would follow her around. She said the language it used was vile and obscene. Then the rest of the family began to hear it too.

With the neighbourhood and indeed further afield hearing about the strange and sinister events, soon everyone wanted to go there to see it for themselves, and newspapers far and wide began to report on the mystifying and inexplicable phenomena occurring at the farm.

One such visitor was a Mr Percy Woodcock. He was an artist, but he also belonged to the American Society for Psychic Research, and he wished to investigate what was happening. He took Dinah aside and asked her, had she heard the voice today? She replied that she had heard the rough man's voice only a few moments earlier, when she had been outside near one of the farm sheds. Mr Woodcock asked her to show him where this was and she accompanied him to it.

No sooner had they arrived at the shed than Mr Woodcock was personally addressed by the invisible entity. He heard the words aloud; "I am the Devil. I will have you in my clutches; Get out of this or I'll break your neck!"

The researcher was stunned and horrified for a moment or too but then found his own voice. He bravely chastised the entity for such threats. However, the response he received was an utterance of even more vile threats from 'the devil.'

A weird message too had also been found scrawled on one of the walls in recent days. "You gave me fifteen cuts," it said.

The researcher came up with the idea of providing a

piece of paper and a pencil and invited the spirit to write on it. According to both the researcher and the girl, after a few moments the pencil lifted in the air by an unseen hand. Apparently, the message was as perhaps expected; it was full of curses and threats.

A voice then said, "I'll steal your pencil." Then the pencil was hurled across the yard. The researcher, in an effort to rule out the possibility that the young girl could perhaps be "throwing" her voice, instructed her to fill her mouth with water so that she would not be able to talk.

The gruff and deep male voice rang out once more, and it was obvious that this voice was not coming out of Dinah. The conversation, apparently between man and devil, continued for several hours.

Prior to this psychic investigator Mr Woodcock's visit, Mr Dagg had gone to see a local woman called Elizabeth Barnes, for help. She had the reputation for being a 'Seer,' who was possessed with the ability of second sight. Her nickname was "The Witch of Plum Hollow." She told the father that the cause of his malevolent intruder was because of the actions of a person who lived locally.

She told him that the "black arts" were being used against his family. She said that a woman, a boy, and a girl who lived close-by were using black magic against him and his family. The father thought instantly of a Mrs Wallace, a widow with a young daughter and son. They were embroiled in an ongoing boundary dispute with Mr Dagg.

When the psychic researcher learnt of this dispute and of what the 'wise woman' had said, he questioned the gruff menacing voice about this. The disembodied voice told him instantly that Mrs Wallace had sent him to persecute the Dagg family. The researcher asked the voice when this would stop.

The voice replied that it would not say: "You meddle with the Black Arts. I won't tell you. Shut up. I will break your neck for I am the Devil, the son of the blessed." The voice added that this was just "fun" to him. That he enjoyed it.

The researcher Woodcock decided that he must go to the accused woman and ask her if she really had been casting black magic against the family under siege by this sinister voice. That very evening, he went to her home. He manged to get her to go with him back to the Dagg's cabin. As soon as she arrived there, the sinister voice immediately rang out, for all to hear.

It informed everyone in the room that this woman had used a book "of the black arts," and that after using it, she had hidden it in the swamps. The voice said it was going to leave now, after holding court for a lengthy time, and it said it must say its goodbye to them on the next evening.

When the next evening came, a crowd were ready and waiting for it to appear at the farm. Strangely however, when it appeared it now claimed that it was an Angel. It was the same voice, but it said: "I am sent from Heaven, sent by God, sent to drive that fellow away."

The crowd were so curious that they tested it. One man asked the voice to tell it about a specific secret that no-one else knew. The voice spoke aloud, telling the man's exact secret, and he was dumbstruck – this piece of information had been known only to the man himself and his daughter, who had told him this piece of information on her death-bed.

No-one else knew this information. While most in the crowd now believed they were in the presence of an Angel, the psychic researcher appealed to them, telling them that this voice was the same voice of the creature that had told them he was the devil. At this, the voice lost its sweet nature and exploded in temper, returning to the mannerisms of the entity from prior days who would blaspheme and utter curses and threats of violence.

Interestingly, all of the visitors there that night signed a sheet of paper, testifying to what they had heard and everything that had happened that night. The researcher then left; but more was to come. The devil called for a clergyman to come to the farm, and a minister called Reverend Bell was fetched. The Methodist minister however refused to engage in conversation with 'the devil,' whereupon the voice called him "a coward" and "all words."

Reverend Bell responded by trying to drive the devil out — but the devil did not take him seriously and told him to stick with his day job! Chastised and defeated, the reverend left. After this, the voice told the crowd; "You don't believe I am an Angel because my voice is coarse. I tell the truth." At this, his voice became the sweetest voice they had ever heard, and indeed, began to sing in the most angelic voice they had ever heard.

"Come to the saviour," he sung, "He is calling you to Jesus, come, come to him brothers and sisters." All present later testified that it was the most divine voice they had ever heard. Some were even moved to tears by it.

Then, exactly at 3 a.m., the voice told them it was now departing - but it would return one last time to see the children, tomorrow. Sometime the next morning, the three children ran in from the fields. Mary curiously told her mother; "The beautiful man took Johnny in his arms, he went to Heaven and was all red."

Their mother, very alarmed now, asked her to describe what she saw. The children said that it was a man "dressed in white with ribbons and pretty things" all over his clothing, and stars and gold on his head. His face was 'lovely' with long white hair. They said he had bent down and scooped up the children. He told them that despite what the psychic researcher believed, he was an Angel not the devil, and he would "show him."

The children said that he then rose up from the ground into the air and ascended "to Heaven" in a blaze of fire. No matter who asked the children about this peculiar incident, and no matter how many times they were asked, they never deviated in their retelling of the event.

While some perhaps may have been sceptical of the events caused by this mysterious figure at the farm, the Father's reputation remained intact despite of it, as he went on to become the local Mayor. Dinah was sent away to live with her natural father, as some believed it had been her who had been most afflicted by the entity and indeed some accused her of being behind it, though for the vast majority who had witnessed the encounters, they all knew it had been completely impossible for her to have performed any of these feats herself.

Her whereabouts however became mysteriously unknown, prompting some to believe the rumour that she somehow 'disappeared' by this malevolent discarnate spirit who had besieged her at the Farm.

According to local historian Greg Graham, there are no marriage or death records for her on file anywhere. Added to this is the local story that she worked as a teenager on a different farm, where she was called upon by a mysterious man one night, and never seen again..... Was this the 'devil' returning to lay claim to her...?

Chapter Fourteen

'Gef' the ghost

"**I**'m a freak. I have hands and I have feet, and if you saw me, you'd faint, you'd be petrified, mummified, turned into stone."

These were the words of 'Gef', the strangest entity, that bewildered a farming family and most of the United Kingdom when his story was reported on across many city newspapers.

"It is impossible to deny that there is serious evidence … for Gef's reality," said Mr. R.S. Lambert of the BBC, in the 1930's. We could be forgiven for believing that Gef was a man, or a boy, but in fact 'Gef' was an animal, an animal that appeared not quite of this world.

The closest in description of 'Gef' or 'Jeff' was apparently a mongoose. That could talk. Mongoose is the English name for family of Herpestidae, who are small carnivores native to Eurasia, Africa, and Southern Europe, and are visually similar to Meerkats. They have long bodies, long angular faces and short legs with a tail. They were venerated in ancient Egypt for their ability to handle venomous snakes. 'Gef,' who was most colloquially called 'Jeff,' also took on other appearances too – varying from a strange cat, something that looked a bit like a pig, and other indefinable small monsters.

Mostly though, 'Jeff' was invisible. He appeared on the Isle of Man at a small and isolated farm, Doarlish Cashmen, owned by 58-year-old Mr. T. Irving, a former travelling piano salesman. Mr. Irving himself was somewhat of an anomaly, for although he owned the farm, he did not work it and remained always immaculately suited with uncalloused hands.

He and his wife had a 12-year-old daughter called Voirrey, who was known to wander the Moors alone except accompanied by her dog Mona. It was said that the dog would hypnotise a rabbit with mesmerism while the child sneaked up on the rabbit from behind and clubbed it to death!

The Isle of Man Newspaper wrote: 'The spook or buggane has chosen an ideal spot. No lonelier place could be found ...isolated from the outside world ..up a narrow lane. The buggane as we shall call this creature has set aflame the fumes of fancy; an evil spirit has taken possession.

The family's farmhouse was up a steep desolate hill and two miles from the nearest village. It was a small affair with no running water and no electricity. It had stone walls and small windows and lined with thick wood panelling on the inside. This gave the house some insulation from the cold winds and there was a gap between the walls as a result of the panelling. The story of Jeff began when the family started hearing knocking from inside of the house.

Not only were there knocks coming at all hours from the house, but there seemed to be no explanation about what could be causing the knocks. It was not the sound of rats or mice scurrying around. It was not anyone knocking on the walls from outside – for the father checked repeatedly and never found anyone standing outside of the house.

It wasn't just knocking though – there was wild and terrifying growling, barking, gurgling sounds, and even more strangely, frequent blowing sounds. At other times it sounded like a gurgling baby trying to say its first words. These odd bodily noises began to be heard at all hours of the day and night, and yet they could find no source to explain where the animal sounds were coming from.

In an endeavour to try to work out the mystery of the puzzling noises, the farmer decided to make noises against the walls himself. To his surprise, whatever noises he made, whether grunts or gurgles, the same noises came back from behind the wood panelling. Then it began spitting at them.

Very disturbed by this, and concerned for the safety of his wife and daughter, Mr. Irving set a number of traps, in an attempt to catch the perpetrator, whatever it turned out to be, although he could not for the life of him understand how barking and growling and even giggling could be coming from the tiny spaces between the walls and the wood panelling – the gap was certainly not big enough to host any animal large enough to growl.

Nevertheless, he set a number of traps and laid down poison to catch the creature. This had no effect however and proved entirely fruitless. The noises continued unabated. Some nights it kept them awake until 3 am with incessant chatter.

In exasperation one day, the famer exclaimed, "What in the name of God can he be?" To which he received the reply, or rather a voice, mimicking him; "What in the name of God can he be?" The voice was in falsetto tone, in an octave higher than a woman's voice.

After Mr. Irving recovered from his shock, he determined to carry out some experiments with whatever creature remained hidden behind the panelling. For a start, he began reciting come of his daughter's nursery rhymes. The creature responded by reciting them back to him, word for word. It was even capable of the creature reciting the rhymes reciting them backwards, perfectly, with no difficulty at all. It would sing the nursey rhymes as though it had always known them, completely fluently.

The creature announced that it had always been able to talk, but that it had started with animal grunts and growls to get the family acclimatised to its presence. "It announces its presence now by calling myself or my wife by our Christian names."

The creature most liked being in the ceiling rafters above the stairs. Its voice seemed most often to come from there now. Yet the family still could not visibly see it there at all. Then it began to mimic the family's conversations, reciting them back to the family. No matter where in the house the family talked to each other, the creature appeared to be able to hear them and parrot it back at them. Even when the family whispered to each other, astoundingly the creature repeated it all back to them.

With still no idea what this creature looked like, the father said, "It's hearing powers are phenomenal. It is no use whispering. It detects the whisper 15-20 feet away, tells you that you are whispering, and repeats it exactly."

Not only that, but Jeff seemed to have an uncanny ability to tell them gossip that would later turn out to be true. He said that he often left the house and travelled on the bus or in the backseat of cars belonging to the other Islanders, and he heared things on his travels. He would tell them all manner of private things, which in time would come out in gossip from the other residents of the Island and what he had told them would always be scandalously correct.

As time went on, Jeff eventually allowed the family to 'feel' him. On a few occasions, he allowed them to put their hand up through the ceiling rafters and touch his fur. He even let them feel his tiny sharp teeth once. They gave him food – bacon, sausages, and chocolate; but he would not eat their eggs. For some reason he just didn't like them.

In kind, as a gesture of gratitude to the family, he would kill rabbits in the fields for them and leave them to be found. He apparently preferred to kill them with

169

his bare hands! By strangulation. Although, the Manx Newspapers said, 'He has been seen in many forms and resembles many animals. With the body of a weasel or a cat and a pig's head with great glowing eyes, hissing breath and a high-pitched voice.'

Although it seemed that Jeff was intending no harm to the family, and seemed to be simply a playful prankster, it must have been a little alarming to find the strangled rabbits. When he'd first made his appearance known in the farmhouse, Mr. Irving had been concerned for the safety of his daughter.

Jeff had a habit of throwing things, heavy things, that would go flying through the air. And he displayed a fondness for throwing things in Voirrey's room in particular. Mr. Irving had felt it necessary to remove his daughter from her bedroom and move her into the bedroom he shared with his wife. Once tucked into bed with her parents, a powerful force on the other side of the door bent the door inwards, causing it to bulge wildly as if it would give and break. Then came Jeff's high-pitched voice; 'I'm coming in!'

Wrote the Peel City Guardian; 'Many who have listened, have, at the sound of his voice, felt the felt the hair rising and the spine shivering – sure signs of the presence of the unnatural.'

In fact, the father tried to kill Jeff with a gun – but this of course had not been effective, because he could not see Jeff. Jeff's response to the gun had been to unleash ungodly screams that nearly shattered the family's eardrums, so affronted was Jeff by this threat of violence to him. Jeff retaliated with his words too, threating imminent violence to the family if Mr Irving did not cease. In fact, it was some weeks before hostilities ceased and Jeff stopped issuing the family with threats.

Jeff threatened more than just the family on occasions. Charles Morrison, a life-long pal of the father, described the time he heard Jeff shouting; "Tell Arthur Morrison (Charles's father) not to come. I won't speak if he does come. I'll blow his brains out." This was followed by the sounds of heaving, pounding and thumping from behind the wood panelling, and the pounding was coming from more than one place – it was coming from all corners of the house, at the same time.

He told the family once; "I am not evil. I could be if I wanted to be. You don't know what damage or harm I could do if I were roused. I could kill you all."

A Captain M. H. Macdonald, who was a businessman and a racing car driver, visited the farm on several occasions. One day, he and Mr. Irving walked a distance of four miles to the village of Peel where they had lunch and a pint of beer. They chatted idly on their walk and for some reason the topic of Mrs. Irving's shoes came up.

When they returned home later to the farm, Mrs. Irving greeted them at the front door and was able to describe their exact conversation on the topic of her shoes – because Jeff had already told her. The men agreed, she had recalled what they said most precisely. The captain was also treated to a game of 'heads or tails' with Jeff, who tossed the coin through an opening of the wooden panels.

In one incident, a gang of workmen carrying out road repairs watched in astonishment as a piece of bread one of them had thrown away into the field, appeared to be moving on its own across the field. On another occasion, a cousin of the father was working tilling in a field when he felt stones being thrown at him – yet he could see no perpetrator.

Jeff grew fond of Voirrey though – it was said that he would follow the wild child out onto the moors and throw stones at anyone she met on her walks. He guarded her jealously and it was said that he had a remarkably accurate aim when he hit people with the stones. Soon, hundreds of rabbits would begin to be found, their bodies lying strewn across the moors and fields. Jeff said he did this so that the family could eat the rabbits or sell them to other islanders for profit. His preferred method of killing was to strangle the rabbits!

In time, Jeff told the Irving's that he had come from India, where he said he had often been shot at by farmers. He said that he had lived with a man who wore a green turban on his head. He explained that he had then travelled with a man named 'Holland' from India onto Egypt, and then from Egypt he had arrived in England.

He declared that he had been born in 1852 on June 7th. This would make him 83 years of age. He also said that he came from "the fifth dimension." On another occasion he said, "I am the Holy Ghost." At other times, he declared himself an ordinary ghost and threatened; "I will haunt you with clanking chains."

As the months passed, his mischievous behaviour continued. He bit Mrs Irving's finger when she pocked it though the wood panels. He would regularly lock the daughter in her room from the outside. He would laugh raucously whenever he found out any new gossip to tell them, or when the gossip was later revealed to be true.

He would hurl their furniture across rooms just for the fun of it. He seemed to have the power of telekinesis – able to make objects move of their own accord. He also began to show himself, just occasionally, to the family.

At first, he told them; "I might let you see me some time, but thou wilt never get to know what I am!" His first appearance seemed to be accidental, and happened when the daughter, Voirrey, hid outside and caught a fleeting glimpse of him.

Then he showed himself standing in the rafters of the ceiling. In fact, he even allowed them to photograph him once – although he declared himself to be very nervous, and they found he could not stand still. The black and white photographs came out too blurry.

For those who were granted the privilege of seeing him, they described his appearance as a bit like a squirrel, with a long bushy tail and light brown fur, small ears and a "pushed-in face." His little front paws were described as "hand-like" with 3 fingers and a thumb. No mammal yet discovered has 3 fingers and a thumb though. He was also described as appear like a cat, or a pig's head with great glowing eyes, hissing breath and a high-pitched voice.

Jeff's strange existence at the farm reached mainland

England and the newspapers sent reporters to the tiny island. A reporter for the Manchester Daily Dispatch wrote that they heard Jeff talk to them. A newspaper from the United States even offered Jeff a sum of $50,000 to come and tour the country. (This was a huge sum of money in those days.)

Famed British paranormal investigator Harry Price took a journey to the island to investigate. He brought with him a reporter, Mr. R.S. Lambert of the B.B.C. Lambert would later win libel damages in a courtroom from accusers who declared there was no truth to this mysterious creature and that Lambert was 'deranged.' The court, for its part, took the view that Lambert's investigation of Jef wasn't a sign of madness, and he was awarded him the substantial sum of £7500 in damages. The case was even discussed in the House of Lords.

Sadly, for Lambert and Price however, when they were given a fur sample said to have come from Jeff, it did disappoint them when it turned out, according to the Zoological Society who analysed it, to be most likely sheep dog hair. Photos taken by the Society for Psychical Research were unable to prove his existence too – their quality varied and were indistinct. On the other hand, the Irving's told investigators, and apparently Jeff himself said, that he did not want to show himself to investigators for fear they would capture him and take him away for examination.

In a 1932 interview with the *Manchester Daily Dispatch*, James described Jeff as "a little animal resembling a stoat, ferret, or weasel." How could a weasel throw furniture across a room, make a door bulge as though it were about to break, strangle hundreds of rabbits with its 'hands'? And speak in multiple languages? Yet the investigators spoke to many witnesses all who testified that this was no hoax, and they themselves felt convinced that this was something so out of the ordinary as to be wholly inexplicable. They wondered though, could he be the result of a bizarre Folie à Deux, or a mass delusion among the trio living there?

They were also disappointed that Jeff never showed

himself to them. Jeff explained this as being due to the fact that he was afraid of being captured. "They would put me in a bottle!" he declared. Another esteemed investigator, Dr Nandor Fodor of the Society for Psychical Research, a trained psychoanalyst, also became convinced that Jeff was indeed genuine. Fodor considered the idea of Jeff as akin to a witches' familiar.

He grew shy of being around when reporters or investigators came. As soon as they'd gone however, he would return to his fun again. Though he was closer to the family now, and they seemed to tolerate his cohabitation, without the ongoing threats from him, he would still hurl insults at them when he felt like it. One time, when the father was reading his newspaper quietly, Jeff shouted; "Read it out, you fat-headed gnome!" He said he did this, "for devilment!" The Isle of Man newspapers called him 'The Spook of Dalby," or 'The Buggane."

Over half a century after Jeff's occupation of the remote and isolated farmhouse, Voirrey maintains this was no hoax. She wished that there were, for all the disadvantageous publicity it attracted into her family's life, but she is adamant that Jeff existed. Interviewed by Fate magazine in the 1970's, she told them she was labelled as being "mental" and her life made a misery because of it.

Of Jeff, she said "His voice was very high-pitched. He swore a lot. At first, he talked to me more than anyone. We carried on regular conversations. It was not a hoax. But I do wish he had left us alone. I wish it had never happened. I had to leave the Isle of Man. We were snubbed. The other children used to call me "The Spook." Gef has even kept me from getting married," she says.

For those who say it was a clever hoax and the daughter must have been a talented ventriloquist performing 'parlour tricks,' it seems that many witnesses said they heard the voice of Jeff when she was no -where near the house. In fact, 18 people signed statements, according to the Isle of Man Examiner, that they had witnessed unaccountably strange things happen in the house.

The voice of Jeff would often sound as though it was coming from different parts of the house at the same time. How did Jeff do that? And how did he literally strangle hundreds of rabbits?

180

Chapter Fifteen:

The 'Tower of the Ghosts.'

On the subject of Gnomes, where in our last story Jeff called Mr. Irving 'A fat-headed gnome,' in this next story it appears to feature gnomes with a very sinister agenda. The story is called the 'Tower of the Ghosts,' as it is known in Buenos Aires, Argentina, and it involves the curious and disturbing tale of the death of a beautiful artist at the hands of vengeful gnomes.

The 'Ghost Tower' is the top section of a stunning Catalan modernist building located on the cross-section of Wenceslao Villafañe, Benito Pérez Galdós and Almirante Brown, in the La Boca neighbourhood of Buenos Aires. It was built by Maria Luisa Auvert Arnaud, a wealthy ranch owner. However, the wealthy rancher stayed for just one year and left this majestic property mysteriously, without any explanation.

The building was then converted into individual rental

apartments and among the new tenants was a very beautiful woman called Clementina. She was a quiet woman who kept herself to herself and worked quietly from her apartment as an artist. Her apartment was situated up in the atelier tower.

She would spend all day in the tower, painting. Sometimes people, men especially, would watch her as they sat drinking coffee in the café opposite her building. They say that passers-by could not stop admiring the beauty of her windows, even more so when they saw her.

Clementina left her apartment only to attend the Faculty of Arts where she was studying painting. Her artwork was getting noticed, and one day a journalist visited her to interview her. The journalist Eleanor, spent time talking to her, looking at her paintings, and taking photographs of them. Then the journalist left, satisfied she had captured the artist and her work very well, and feeling excited to write up her article.

After the journalist had the photographs developed, she

sat looking at them, and she was stunned to see something completely inexplicable in one of the photos. It appeared that in this particular photograph of one of Clementina's paintings, she could see three small, mysterious beings who were definitely not in the painting when she had taken the photographs. She thought her eyes had to be deceiving her and yet she could not deny that there really did appear to be three very strange little creatures in the photo. They looked like goblins, or gnomes.

Without wasting time, she went to Clementina's house to show her what she had discovered. The painter was surprised to see her again, but she was even more surprised when she saw the three creatures. Clementina immediately refused to talk about it. Appearing very disturbed, she invited the journalist to leave her house immediately and said quietly as the journalist left; "You did not have to see them." The journalist left, very confused by the artist's behaviour and still disturbed by the appearance of these strange creatures.

In the days and nights that followed, several of the

neighbours thought they heard screams coming from the tower. They brushed it off as their imagination. Then one night, the normally quiet and calm building was awoken to the sound of blood-curdling screams. The screams were coming from the tower, where Clementina lived.

When the residents rushed up to investigate, they found her apartment empty but outside on the sidewalk, her body lay bloodied and dead. It appeared that Clementina had committed suicide, throwing herself out of the tower to certain death. She had died instantly.

Her tragic death was written about in the city newspapers, and the journalist who had interviewed her just the day before was so shocked when she read it. The artist had given no indication of being depressed or distressed about anything that could have caused her to throw herself to death from the tower.

In fact, her close circle of friends said she had confided in them about how excited she was; the painting she was soon to finish was her best, she had said. It had taken her years to paint, but she knew this was a turning point in her career – this would be her most famous painting, when she finished it.

Of course, the journalist could not forget the strange attitude of the artist when she had returned to show her the photographs. The artist had refused to talk about it. Unable to stop thinking about this and the subsequent terrible tragedy, the journalist went to the apartments to investigate, asking the artist's neighbours about the life of the artist and about whether they had ever seen anything they couldn't explain what had happened that night.

After talking to some of Clementine's neighbours, all she had discovered was that the wealthy former owner of the building had left in what seemed to be a hurry but had given no explanation for abandoning the beautiful and expensive building that she had commissioned to be built for her. The journalist determined to visit the former owner and try to find out more.

She located Maria Luisa Auvert Arnaud and she heard the most fantastic and mysterious account imaginable. Mrs Arnaud began by asking the journalist if she believed in goblins, to which the journalist replied an unsure, "No."

Then Mrs Arnaud began to narrate an ancient legend of Catalonia, which says that in the forests of the Pyrenees live the "follets," or, little goblins, that always sleep in the mushrooms. Mrs. Arnaud said that while living there in her home with the gnomes, they collaborated with the servants, and were helpful every day but that one day, one of the gnomes tried to make a pass at a maid and one of the male servants standing close beside the maid, took hold of the gnome and threw it against the wall to remove it from the maid's company.

Understandably, the gnome was infuriated and from that day forth, all hell broke loose in the household. The gnomes were now at war. Furniture would be hurled across rooms, legs of chairs were severed, knives flew wildly through the air, embedding them wherever they landed, and of course, seriously jeopardizing the lives of the servants and their mistress.

Mrs Arnaud confided in the journalist that she and her servants had felt they had no choice but to leave her dream home because they were being harassed by these small malevolent characters who lived among the mushrooms that had been brought from Catalonia.

However, that was all she would say. She refused to go into any more detail. But she looked terrified when she had talked. She made the journalist swear that she would not breathe a word of her tale, for fear that she would be forced into a lunatic asylum and her assets would be seized.

When Mrs. Arnaud had moved into her new home in the city, on all of the balconies she had put exotic plants from Catalonia, that she had specially brought for her new home. Among the plants, appeared to be a type Mushroom; some species of course are edible, while others are hallucinogenic. Had these exotic mushrooms somehow got into her system and she had hallucinated that there were strange small monsters coming after her? And yet, it didn't seem that she had actually eaten any of the mushrooms, but rather they had been decorative.

For some reason, it seems that the beautiful artist may have unwittingly upset the gnomes – or perhaps they were just looking to take vengeance on anyone who now lived there. Current residents have told people that items in their apartments mysteriously disappear. Then turn up in an entirely different place at a later point in time or are never found again.

One of the things that disappeared forever was also the mysterious painting by Clementina, that the journalist had photographed with three gnomes standing in the painting. Presumably, they did not want their existence captured for immemorial. Had they managed to drive Clementine to suicide? As a punishment for the error of capturing them on camera? - For the previous owner, Mrs. Arnaud, had confided that she had been forced to leave to save her own life and that of her servants too.

Chapter Sixteen

"Come to Us"

In the early hours of the morning on November 27th 1992, Spanish police visited a number 8 Lius Marin Street in Madrid, having been summoned by the father of the family who lived there, the Guterrez Lazaru's, and this would begin the tale of a saga which defied both scientific and logical explanations, and it remains one of the most perplexing cases in the annals of parapsychology. The Madrid police will soon find themselves, by their own testimonies, terrified, after a death that is unexpected and unexplainable.

Tt seems the cursed saga all began as a naive game; one which thousands if not millions before have played. It began as a result of playing the Ouija board. The daughter, Estefania, 18, had played the Ouija with her friends, and it would not be long before she was dead. They had done this as they wanted to try to make contact with the boyfriend of one of them who had sadly died in a motorbike accident.

After playing, Estefania became possessed by 'El Mal;' Pure evil. She began to hear voices, see dark shadows. Things would move by themselves, particularly the crucifixes in the family home. By the time her father called the police, she had already mysteriously died.

Chief Inspector Jose-Pedro Negri and five other police officers found her father standing outside in the street, despite the cold of the November night. When the policemen asked to enter the house, he reluctantly led them inside. The father began to explain that his daughter had died mysteriously some weeks earlier. As he talked to them, a closet door in the room burst open suddenly and violently.

"Totally unnaturally," the police report later said, and for them, this was just the beginning of the night. From somewhere outside the house came a loud noise and it sounded as though it were coming from the terrace. When they cautiously approached the terrace and looked out, no-one was there. Moments later they noticed a brownish-coloured fluid had appeared on the small table that housed the telephone, which looked to be consistent with "drool." "There was no obvious source from which this could have come."

As they walked around the other rooms in the house, they saw that a crucifix on the wall had been separated from Christ, as though hands had pulled them apart. Beside the crucifix were scratches on the wall. Four of the policemen left, preferring to wait outside in the cold rather than stay a moment longer in the house. Only Inspector Jose Negri and one other officer remained.

The father told them that on one occasion, one of his sons was thrown across the room in front of him by something he could not see. When the police inspector entered the bathroom, an ice-cold chill flooded through his body. "It was a cold that I had never felt before." The family told him they often heard disembodied voices coming from the bathroom, when no-one was inside. The Inspector said that what he witnessed that night seemed to be "Of diabolical origin."

"I sat down in the bedroom to see if anything would happen. We heard a terrible scream behind us which came from the small balcony. I quickly opened the door and ran out to see if I could see anything there but there was nothing. The noise was dreadful. When I'd first entered the bedroom, I'd noticed a large crucifix on the wall and hanging off it was a smaller crucifix like one a child would get at communion. A few minutes later the crucifix had been turned upside down and the little crucifix was on the floor. The door had three or four deep scratches on it as if someone had clawed it deep into the door."

The mother and father told the Inspector about the strange death of their daughter; a death they believed had now brought terrible wrath upon the house. She had been found in bed convulsing violently and screaming in agony and terror. Her parents had her rushed to hospital, but she never recovered from the coma and died in hospital. A few months before this, in March 1990, Estefania and her friends had played with a Ouija board while at college at the Institute Companeras.

Accounts say that when the Students' teacher discovered them playing with it, she seized the board and threw the glass they had been using as a pointer, to the ground, shattering it into hundreds of shards of glass. The glass had, just moments before, been mysteriously full of smoke, and when it was shattered on the ground the smoke went up into Estefania's nose. This was corroborated by the teacher present.

Since that moment, the girl became a changed girl, it was said. She would begin to say that there were dark figures watching her from the hallway of her home, and these figures began to call her name. She described the dark figures as a group of tall, thin, famished people who would raise their arms and shake their fists and urge her; "Come to us, Come to us."

It was not long after playing with the Ouija that Estefania began to have hallucination and seizures. She would snarl at her brothers and growl or bark like a wild dog. She was plagued by "strange and evil" people who stalked her in the house. During the last weeks of her life, her seizures grew in frequency. At night, she said the voices were relentless. She would get no sleep. On occasions, her body appeared to have almost super-human strength.

She would become suddenly enraged, furious and frightening, screaming at her brothers and sister in a voice which no longer sounded like her own. She sounded like an evil man, or worse, a demon itself. The voice was deep, gravely, hoarse and nothing like her own and it would hurl the vilest insults and threats. Her parents became desperate to find out what was wrong with her their daughter, who had changed beyond any recognition.

She was now having terrible seizures in which she would thrash violently and then sink into a catatonic state. They took her to the doctor, who referred her to hospital specialists who conducted numerous tests. The tests found nothing, and the specialists could make no diagnosis to explain her behaviour.

One night, her father was lying in bed when he suddenly felt something pinning him down and touching his hands and feet outside the blanket. At first, he thought it felt like the hands of his children, but it gave him the most chilling feeling at the same time. Later, he would see that she was fast asleep in her own bed. As the strange and unexplained incidents continued to happen, the father became so uncomfortable being in the house with his family that he had movement sensors installed throughout the house.

Estefania and her sister were by this point all sleeping together, as if to protect themselves from the nightly intrusions. On one occasion, as they slept huddled together, they were woken by the sounds of something in the hallway beyond stood a dark figure. As they stared at it, it began crawling on the floor, very slowly, coming into their room.

One of her sisters said, "We heard a whistling sound, like on other nights, and then a groan near the door. We were so scared we were frozen. It was then we noticed something on the floor as the light from the streetlamps lit up our room, and it was the shape of a man crawling, dragging itself along the floor. He had black head, no eyes, no mouth; nothing. It was crawling toward us. Toys we had on a shelf started to be thrown violently towards the other wall, one by one, and then we heard shouts." They found themselves pinned against the wall by their wrists.

Then she died. On August 14th, she was admitted to hospital as an emergency in a coma. She never recovered. Her brothers, now in their forties ,say that their experiences were exaggerated; that their sister had epilepsy, and that this ran in their family; but it has to be asked, if that were the case, the doctors at the hospital who undertook all manner of tests on her would surely have diagnosed that if it were the case? The banging, like huge fists pounding on their walls, continued after her death.

The grotesque laughter that they heard inside the house continued, as well as the dark shadows stalking them. They'd resorted to barricading themselves inside rooms by piling furniture against the doors in an attempt to keep out the evil infiltrating their home; but this was futile. Still the door handles would sinisterly twist, invisible fists would pound on the door, their furniture would be flung back from the door.

The unexplained phenomena continued unabated. Her father had lain flour across the rooms and when he checked back, he found footprints like the size of a large man's shoes. Doors were still opening and slamming violently on their own. Electrical devices would switch themselves on or off with no human nearby. Decorative objects such as photos and picture frames and crucifixes would seem to come alive.

On one occasion, a hanging photo of Estefania appeared to have burnt, yet the frame and glass were still intact. The photos had been found laying on the floor, yet the photo frame and glass were still hanging on the wall completely undamaged. Things got so bad that the father tried to kill himself, several times, and after this, he felt the only way to escape from the evil was to leave the house...

Chapter Seventeen

Water ghosts

Donald Worley was an investigator into all things paranormal. He dedicated his life to his investigations and in this following case, it would seem he went above and beyond.

"My reputation stands behind my statement that this is not fiction but fact. I present the unbelievable details in the form of an urgent letter I wrote to the Sheriff of Wayne County and the Palladium Newspaper, Richmond, Indiana, January 6th, 1998.

'Dear Sirs, yet another child drowning in your area of Dublin and Centerville; it is urgent that you listen very carefully. I must somehow convince you: You are faced with a SERIAL KILLER in your area! This insidious thing preys on children and what is more terrible is it is not a visible person that you can track down. But read on! There is hope something can be done.

We are not talking about coincidence here. It was the crash of two automobiles north of the iron bridge over Simmons Creek that gave birth to all of this. My informants are a Mr. and Mrs Herman, 67 and 65. It was Mr Herman's brother's wife who was killed in the accident. The husband, wife, two sons and the 18-month-old baby were returning from a swimming party in Simmons Creek in the summer of 1937. The crash threw the mother and her baby in her arms out of the car. In her last fleeting moment, the mother raised her head, looked for her baby, moaned, then died.

The baby was unhurt. Apparently, this mother's great love for her baby became a twisted, destructive thing. In disembodied form she has never ceased to seek to replace that which she thinks she lost. In her frenzy to have her baby back, this tragically mixed-up soul probably created more events.'

He continues, 'The Jana Hunter, 8 years old, drowning in 1963. This incident gives us some important clues about what is going on. For some time, Jana talked about an angel that would appear to her. She was told that she would not grow up like other girls and have babies but instead was going to go with the angel. This proved to be correct when she drowned in a limestone drop off in Simmons Creek below the iron bridge.

The father was able to rescue his pregnant wife and son when they became hysterical and fell in when Jana did, but he reached Jana too late. The mother claimed that she had seen Jana grow calm, look up, and smile before going under for the final time. Apparently, something controlled the little girl's mind at the crucial time.'

'On a cold winter night in February 1968, an automobile approached the bridge and the four witnesses first thought the object was a big dog about to cross the highway. Then, illuminated by the car headlights, it became apparent that it was a form of a person dressed in a long flowing garment. The driver swerved as the light appeared to form a slender shape of what appeared to be a woman moving in slow steady motion. They heard a low whispering cry.'

Worley also mentions two other strange drownings,

reported in the Indianapolis press: 'James Hogan Jr., 18, and his cousin, Michael Phillips, 21, both of Indianapolis, died in the White River at Indianapolis Sunday. Hogan's father drowned in Fall Creek at Indianapolis in 1958 trying to retrieve a turtle.

Hogan's mother, Mrs. Thomas Johnson Sr., said the family had gone to fish in the river when her younger son lost his bobber while casting from shore. She said she warned him not to go after it, "but he was already on his way." When he was about halfway out, she said, "It seemed as if something were pulling him under, like a current. He kept holding his hand up and then Michael went to save him and also got in trouble. Now they're both gone..."

In another incident, 'In June 1972, the Tuft children drowning; all four children of Mrs Tutt out playing drowned in a farm pond.' And, in April 1983, 18-month-old Jeremy Rose drowning; 'This son of Sondra Rose was found drowned in a pond outside his home.'

'Concerning these drownings,' Worley says, 'I have a dreadful feeling that there may be any number of other deaths.'   He blames the mother of the first drowning incident for the subsequent drownings - the spirit of the dead woman who believes her baby drowned, now snatches those who go swimming in the water where it happened and indeed other bodies of water nearby; she is now a disembodied serial killer, says Worley.

'This mother's great love for her baby became a twisted, destructive thing. In disembodied form she has never ceased to seek to replace that which she thinks she lost. In her frenzy to have her baby back, this tragically mixed-up soul probably created more events.'

Unfortunately for Donald Worley, neither the Sheriff nor the Newspaper he contacted got back to him...

Chapter Eighteen

FATED

At 11 pm on the eve of July 23rd, 1987, 16-year-old Kathy Hobbs told her mom she was going to the local store. She loved to read romance novels and she said to her mom, "I'm going down to the store and buy a book. Give me a kiss before I go."

Her mom says she asked her, "Why — I'll be up when you get back?" Kathy told her she'd probably stop and talk to some friends when she was out, so her mom might have gone to bed by the time she got back. "So, I gave her a kiss. And that was the last time I saw her," said her mom. Kathy's bloodied body was found in the desert, 11 days later.

It was common for Kathy to go to the store. Her mom said she often walked the 1 1/2 blocks at night to get to the local supermarket. Usually her friends would be around too — at their apartments or at the pool, so her mom did not worry about her daughter going out in the dark. As time went on and her daughter didn't come back, her mother thought no more of it and went to bed. She fell quickly asleep but at 3 am exactly, she was woken up by a very vivid dream.

"I felt like I'd been hit on the head. I woke up out of a sound sleep. Then suddenly, I got a very peaceful feeling and thought, 'Oh well, it's over now,' and I fell back to sleep." When she got up the next morning, she realized her daughter had not come home the night before; her bedroom was empty. This was not normal. Her mom called the police.

Metro Homicide detective lieutenant Kyle L. Edwards led the investigation into her daughter's disappearance. "We tracked down her friends within 24 hours and by the end of day 2, we were convinced she'd probably been abducted." Her picture was circulated heavily across the media. Her mother was desperately worried. She did not have the support of Kathy's father – they'd divorced when Kathy was 8. Kathy's childhood had not been idyllic and what's more, she appeared to be a sombre girl at heart. Perhaps it was also because her friend in middle school had died from a heart condition. "This affected Kathy very much – it was one of the main reasons we moved to LA – to give her a fresh start." Kathy made frequent claims that she herself would never make it to the age of 16.

It appears that though she had a circle of friends, Kathy preferred to spend time in her bedroom, not going out. On her 16th birthday, she told her mom she was very surprised to have made it to 16 and not died. In fact, if anything, this seemed to give her a new lease of life; she now seemed to go out more and socialise more. She'd turned a new leaf. But now she had vanished. She was the last person her mother would imagine running away though. She was far too much of a homebody.

After she disappeared, police made a startling discovery. In her bedroom drawers, they found a series of letters and in these letters, Kathy was explaining that she did not want to upset her mom, but she knew she would not live past 16. The police didn't know what to make of it.

At the store, the supermarket clerk remembered Kathy coming in, and the receipts showed that Kathy had purchased a paperback novel at a quarter after 11 that night. Her body was found 11 days after she disappeared. Rick Pacult was hiking out in the desert near Lake Mead, intending to look for crystals when he suddenly smelled a terrible odour. He walked to where the smell was strongest and there, he saw the body of the 16-year-old.

Tire prints at the scene indicated a vehicle had pulled up, then turned and left. Two rocks near her body were blood - stained. According to the coroner, her death was determined to have been caused by multiple savage blows to her head with the two rocks.

Her mother had been woken from her sleep that night by what felt like a blow to her head! Then there were Kathy's own letters; each one addressed to a separate member of her family. She'd dated the letters when she wrote them, and they'd been written just 4 weeks before she had been murdered.

To her mom she wrote;

'Dear Mother, In the event of my death, you should get this letter. I don't want you to dwell on my death. You were good to me and nobody could have been a better mother. Keep me alive in your heart, love always.'

3 months to the day of her disappearance, LAPD received an anonymous phone call. It was picked up on their answer machine and it was the voice of a man who claimed to have seen Kathy being grabbed by a man in front of the store. She was screaming, he said. He told police he'd written the license plate number down at the time; but when they tried to trace the vehicle, it didn't exist.

Her murder remains officially unsolved, although the police firmly believe she was killed by executed Serial Killer Michael Lee Lockhart, because blue fibres from the crime scene matched fibres in a car he'd stolen during the same time she had disappeared, and credit card receipts place him in the area.

The strangest thing about the case of course is her belief that her fate was to die at 16 and then she did; but also, her mother's dream too - who seemed to physically feel her daughter being killed, who seemed to feel it when her daughter was hit in the head. How can these things be explained rationally other than by otherworldly intervention?

Chapter Nineteen:

Ghost Abductor

In this next strange case, a Reverend Eliakim Phelps moved with his family into The Phelps Mansion in Stratford, Connecticut in 1848. Sometime later, the eldest son vanished. The parents searched the large mansion in a panic but could not find him in any of the rooms.

So they moved their search outside, extending their search into the extensive grounds of the mansion, and it was in the grounds that, to their horror, they discovered their son hanging from a tree, trussed up and bound by a rope. After managing to get him down from the tree, they asked him who had done this to him and his response was that he did not know.

He had no recollection whatsoever about how he had come to find himself trussed up and hanging by a rope from a tree branch. The Reverend was close to the end of his tether, and his nerves by now were thoroughly shredded. You see, this sort of thing had been happening a lot lately.

Reverend Phelps had moved into the Mansion with his second wife and her three young children, having been made a widow earlier, and after his own children had grown up. All was well for the first two years that they lived in the mansion. Then, one Sunday morning, the family returned home from Church to find their house in a peculiar condition.

On their arrival home, they found the front door wide open. The Reverend was certain he had locked it when they had left for Church, and he had the front door key still in his pocket. In the entrance hall, furniture lay strewn, in the study, books were lying on the floor, toys were lying everywhere broken in pieces, and crockery from the kitchen had been smashed all over the floor.

Money that had been left in the house was still there however. Upstairs, his wife's jewellery was also still there, but his wife's nightgown was lain on the bed in a very strange way. The long sleeves of the nightgown had been folded over the chest, reminiscent of the shape a body would be lain out in a coffin.

Odder still, was that a pair of her stockings had been placed at the hem of the nightgown, as if to mimic her legs. Both the Reverend and his wife found themselves profoundly disturbed by the sight of this.

At first, on entrance to their home, the Reverend had presumed that the burglars had run off, that they must have been caught in the midst of the burglary by the family returning home and had run off before they had a chance to steal the valuables. But now, he did not quite know what to think. On inspection of the windows inside the mansion, he could see that none had been broken and none were open.

The family began to clear up the mess and the broken items and later, rather than going to evensong, the Reverend sent his family to Church while he stayed behind. He was clinging to the theory that the burglars, having been disturbed, would return when they expected the Reverend to be at Church, to claim the items they had not had time to steal earlier that day. He hid in the dark in his study, armed with his pistol, waiting for them to return so that he could catch them in the act.

An hour or so passed as he hid, and, growing restless and expectant, he eventually decided to take a tour of the house to see if he could catch the burglars in the act, even though he had heard not a sound all the time he had been hiding in the dark in the study, and, he also knew that all the windows and doors were locked.

Regardless, he still crept out of the study and began to scope each room, and to his complete bafflement, when he entered the drawing room, he froze in shock as he was confronted by a group of effigies, extremely life-like in appearance and form, and they were posed in various forms of devotion, as though in prayer; yet these were not living beings, but rather they were effigies that had been intricately crafted from clothing!

Someone, or, something, had entered his home and

created these praying figures from clothing. Yet he had not heard a sound. Also, the meticulous way in which care had been taken to pristinely create these effigies, it was not something that could have been done in a rush — it would have taken hours of work. Yet all his doors and windows remained closed, and he had heard no footsteps at all. He could find no logical answer to this strange sight in front of his eyes.

This incident, like the earlier one of the nightgowns arranged eerily on the bed, were to be just the beginning of strange times at the Mansion. On many occasions after this, the Reverend and his family returned home to find it appeared as though the house had been ransacked. It went further than this though. Whatever 'it' was that was doing this, as certainly it did not appear to be people, was stepping up its game. It now turned its attention on the family themselves.

And some of the incidents were extremely alarming. On several occasions, the children were lifted up into the air and carried across the room by a pair of invisible hands. All members of the family were physically attacked – sustaining pinches or getting slapped by someone or something that was not visible.

Furniture would be hurled across rooms, food would manifest on the dining room table, windows would break, and knives would fly through the air, making living there rather dangerous. Forks would be twisted in front of them, as though by huge invisible hands. Terrifying sounds would ring out and echo throughout the mansion, day and night. The family became sleep deprived and traumatized. At night, horrifying growls and screams would wake them up. There would be pounding on the walls, loud rapping and bangs.

At breakfast time, kitchen items would fall from above their heads, making them flinch and duck for cover. Then the knives would fly across the room. Upstairs in their closets, clothes would disappear and miraculously appear in another room altogether. Other time, clothes would be ripped to shreds in front of the family, who would be left clinging to each other in terror. Ornaments would be smashed against walls, smashed violently with great force.

Though he was a man of God, the Reverend had a gun; but what good was a gun against an enemy he could not see? An invisible entity or group, who were able to attack with impunity without being seen, who could attack at will at any time? He could offer his family no protection.

The praying effigies would reappear. On one deeply odd occasion, the young children entered their mother's bedroom to see her on her knees praying against the bed. It was only when they got closer that they realized it was not their mother at all; it was a 'model' of their mother made once more from clothing and fashioned into a mannequin to represent their mother.

When word began to spread about the odd things happening inside the Reverend's home, gossip and speculation was the order of the day. Some said that the religious man had been tempted into attending a séance and that this had opened the door to the paranormal and allowed in whatever it was that was terrorizing them.

Others suggested that there was a malevolent ghost by the name of Goody Bassett, who was a woman that had been accused of being a witch and had been hung from a tree close to the Reverend's home in 1651. A reporter from the New York Sun visited and he later wrote an article for the newspaper in which he said that as he sat with the Reverend, his wife, and their eldest daughter in the drawing room, the daughter's arm suddenly began to jerk upwards uncontrollably, like a marionette - as though it was being pulled around by invisible strings

Then she began to cry out in pain, saying that something was poking and pinching her skin. When the newspaper reporter pulled up the long sleeve covering her arm, he discovered that she had deep angry red scratches and marks like those that would be made by fingers. Her skin was raw and inflamed and it was obvious that these were fresh marks on her arm. Another time while asleep in bed, she was woken by a pillow being pressed hard over her face and tape being tied around her neck! She barely escaped with her life.

The New York Sun reported on the 'unaccountable demonstrations of Spirits,' and the editor 'unhesitatingly endorses that these occurrences have taken place' and 'that they seem unexplainable upon any supposition of human agency.'

The Editor of the Bridgeport Standard also visited the mansion to investigate, and he later wrote that when the children were slapped by the invisible thing or things, the sound of the slaps rang out.

The Reverend invited skeptics to his house – including his adult son, who was sure it was some kind of hoax, although he also knew it was not in his father's nature, but he could not bring himself to believe his father's tales about what was going on. On the first night he stayed there, he found himself woken suddenly by the sound of deafening banging. He believed it was coming from the front door of the mansion, but when he got down there, there was no-one standing outside.

Just as he was about to go back upstairs, it happened again and he ran to the door and flung it open but again, no-one was outside. Then banging came from inside the house, sounding like it was coming from upstairs. He bounded up the stairs to catch the person doing it only to again find no-one there.

One day the Reverend was writing at his desk in the study. He was writing a sermon and turned away from his writing for just a moment to contemplate. When he looked back at his writing, he saw that a sheet of paper had appeared in front of him, on which was writing he did not recognize. It was unreadable, indecipherable, and it was certainly not his own writing.

The ink was still wet, but it had not been written by his hand. In the days that followed, other members of the family would also come across sheets of paper, on which was indecipherable writing, words they did not recognize, but as though someone had written personal letters to them. The problem was they had no idea what the letters said.

Sometimes the letters even appeared inside sealed boxes. The Reverend felt that these letters, of which the meaning could not be determined, were from the devil himself or his minions and took them as most likely to be threats of some sort.

A while after this even, the young son of the Reverend disappeared. When they realized he had not been seen for several hours, they searched the house for him but could not find him. Next, they searched the grounds, and to their horror and distress they spotted him hanging from a tree, tied up with rope tight around his neck.

They quickly freed him from his restraints and got him down from the tree and when they asked him what had happened, he told them he had no recollection at all about how he had been tied up and hung from the tree with a rope tight around his neck.

On another occasion, he was discovered inside a closet, again with rope tied tightly around his neck. On several separate occasions he was found in his bedroom lying unconscious on the floor, with no explanation as to what had happened to him.

It was at this point that the Reverend felt he could no longer go on submitting his family to this terrorism from beyond the veil, and although very hesitant and fearful, he decided that his only recourse must be to hold a séance, in an attempt to contact whatever spirit or spirits it was that had no intention of stopping these violent attacks on his family.

With close friends, he attempted the séance and all who were in attendance were shocked that a spirit appeared to have been summoned very fast. The spirit proclaimed that he had once been mortal and he had been a very bad man. He said he had stolen and committed fraud while incarnate and that as a punishment for his crimes he had been banished to Hell for all eternity.

When the Reverend asked him why he was tormenting the family, he told them very simply that he was doing it because it was fun, and he vowed to continue. After the séance, the attacks on the family resumed. Within days the Reverend decided that it was too dangerous for his family to continue to live there any longer and he finally took them away from the vengeful spirit, vowing never to return....

Chapter Twenty

The Clown

A British lady called Trinity contacted me. She'd first contacted me when I mentioned Dan Mitchell's experiences with a Harlequin figure that has stalked him all his life, on a radio show a year or so before our Book 'Desolating Spirits' came out. She was shocked to hear that Dan's experience resembled her own experiences.

This time, she told me the whole story; 'I was in Junior school so I must have been about 8'ish. I saw it twice actually. A year apart. We had a school playing field with a small wooded area to the back of the field. There was power lines just behind the wooded area and that's where I saw him. Weirdly enough he was sat on the power lines. It was awful. I was utterly terrified! It just sat there laughing at me. I'm so shocked that someone else has seen it as well. Anyway, I just thought I'd share that with you. Is Dan the only you've heard of that has seen this thing or are there others as well? Like

I said last year, I've always thought I was the only one who had ever seen one. I was so stunned when I heard it mentioned on a radio show.'

'I was in Velmead Juniors School in Fleet, Hampshire, (England). Now this road and this area is very very strange. That's probably another story, but it may well link with this so I'll give a bit of detail on it. The school is basically built in the woods. If you look on google earth, you'll see what I mean. I lived at the time in a house on Fir Tree Way, almost opposite the school. This backed onto those woods. Those woods are odd.

'Velmead Road has had more than its fair share of deaths. It's not a particularly dangerous road. There's nothing extreme about it. It's just a regular 30-mile an hour road, with woods on one side and houses the other. There is a canal that runs parallel to Velmead Road as well. Water seems to be a good conductor of the abnormal. I have been thinking about trying to work out how many deaths have actually occurred over the years but I remember a good few from my childhood.'

'Anyway, I would have been about 7 or 8. So around '85/'86. It was either late spring or early summer that it happened. I don't recall having a coat on so it must have been warm. It was actually twice that I saw it. Our school has a playing field and at the back was a small strip of trees and behind that power lines ran through. Again, it can all be seen on satellite pictures. I don't recall anything strange leading up to this event. Nothing had happened at home or school. Me and a friend called Susan had found an injured Magpie recently and had tried to nurse it then release it back into the woods.'

'Although this strikes me as odd as I say it - because thinking about it, the Magpie was obviously black and white and so was the clown. We were having a break time, and I was playing in the playground. Someone came running down from what we called the top woods, which was just the trees at the top of the playing field. They said they had found a dead bird. Susan must have been close-by, because we both ran up the field to the top woods because we thought it was our Magpie.

I remember Susan wouldn't let me look at the dead bird

and she held me back; she was shouting at me; "It's not Maggie, it's not Maggie." I think I must have been crying and quite upset at the thought that it was the Magpie. After this, I went to the area where the power lines were. We weren't ever allowed to actually walk under them. The school always had a teacher stationed up there, so we wouldn't do it.'

'I recall something caught my eye and made me look up. There was a Harlequin clown sat, balancing on the power lines. Its suit was the traditional Harlequin black and white diamonds. It appeared male to me. It did have a hat as well and one of those ruffles round its neck. It was rocking slightly and laughing. Not an evil cackle, just normal, almost jolly laughing. I don't think it looked evil; it didn't have any bloody or sharp teeth, nothing like that. I don't recall any odd feelings at the time.'

'I wasn't very impressed to see it and remember fleeing, screaming down the playing field to the playground. Susan was running after me. I remember her asking me why I was screaming. She looked terrified, so I assumed she had seen it. I said something like; "What was that?" but she was actually scared because my screaming had scared her.

When I realized she hadn't seen what I had seen, I don't think that I thought that it wasn't real. I must have thought that she just literally didn't see it because she hadn't looked up. It was so real, I assumed that everyone who was there must have seen it. But they hadn't. It wasn't ghost-like, it was solid. Like a real person dressed as clown somehow sitting on thin power lines.'

'I saw exactly the same thing in exactly the same place a year later. Again, no-one else saw this clown, only me. I recall at the time the whole school seemed to freaked out about something though. There might have been talk of ghosts or something. I remember putting two and two together and realizing that it was exactly a year ago that I'd seen this clown before and that the two must be linked.

In fact, I can still remember the exact moment I made

the link because I was stood in the playground fiddling with a pencil sharpener that I brought on a school trip to Highclere Castle. It was Red and had a picture of an Egyptian mask on it.'

'I never saw the clown anywhere else. I haven't heard all of Dan's story yet but I get the impression that he had a negative experience with it. I wouldn't say mine was positive. I was scared! Very scared, and confused. I'm certain it meant to scare me as well. But it never followed me and the only times I saw it was on those power lines. It was looking at me as well, I forgot to mention that bit. It made eye contact.'

'I have over the years often wondered what it was that saw. I had no Harlequin clown toys or pictures so I'm certain it wasn't just over active imagination. It obviously wasn't a real person. I don't think it was a "ghost" of a person. A demon? A shapeshifter? I literally have no idea.

If you tell people you've seen a ghost, they might not believe you but at least it's a fairly normal thing to say.

Try telling someone you've seen a Harlequin clown and watch their reaction! That's why I almost did my happy dance when I heard about Dan. He probably wasn't dancing for joy but I was. I'm not such a freak anyway! Yippee!'

'It might not be the same thing, but it does seem strange that it presented itself the same. It's such an unusual form to take. Perhaps it's to play on people's fears, but I'm not and never have been scared of any clowns. I admit seeing Harlequin ones can make me a little uncomfortable now, but I'm far from being scared of them. Has anyone else come forward saying they have had an encounter with one?' she asks me.

Chapter Twenty One

Slenderwoman

You've heard of Slenderman right? But have you heard of Slenderwoman? A Japanese legend talks of the 'Hachi Shaku Sama,' which means 'Mrs. eight feet tall.'

One such story goes; 'My grandparents lived in a small village in Japan. Every summer my parents would take me there on holiday to visit them. The last time I saw them was the summer when I was eight years old. My grandparents were inside the house and I was playing by myself outside in the backyard. I heard a strange thumping sound. I didn't know what it was and it was hard to figure out where it was coming from. I started looking around, searching for the source of the noise when I noticed something on top of the tall hedges that enclosed the backyard.

It was a straw hat, but it wasn't resting on the hedge, it was behind it. That's where the sound was coming from. Then, the hat began to move. It stopped at a small gap in the hedge and I could see a face peering through. It was a woman, but the hedges were very high, almost eight feet tall. I was surprised at how tall the woman was. I wondered if she was wearing stilts or some sort of very high-heeled shoes.

Then, just a split second passed and the woman began to walk off and the strange noise disappeared with her, fading as she faded into the distance. Very confused, I got up and ran back into the house. My grandparents were in the kitchen. I quickly sat down with them and told them what I'd seen. They didn't really pay attention - until I described the sound I'd heard - the 'Thump.' Both of them froze. My grandmother's eyes grew big as she put her hand over her mouth. My grandfather looked very serious. He reached for me and grabbed my arm.

"This is very important," he said, with great intensity in his eyes. "How tall was she?"
I replied, "Taller than the garden hedge."
"Where was she standing? When did this happen? What

did you do? Did she see you?" His questions were spit-fire. After I answered him, he left the table and went to the phone and called someone. I couldn't hear what he was saying, but after he finished the conversation, he didn't return to the kitchen. Instead, he walked out the door. Perturbed, I asked my Grandmother what was happening.

"There's something dangerous abducting children in this area," she said. "We call it the 'Hachi Shaku Sama'. It takes on the appearance of an extremely tall woman and in a deep voice makes a thumping sound. A long time ago, it was captured by monks and they managed to confine it in a ruined building on the outskirts of the village, so that it could not escape. But somehow it did. The last time it was seen was 15 years ago."

My grandmother added that anyone who saw it was destined to die within a few days.It sounded so crazy, I wasn't sure I could believe this. When my grandpa came back, there was a really old woman with him. They took me up to my bedroom and my grandpa began covering the windows with sheets of paper that had ancient runes written all over them. The old lady placed salt in the corners of my room. She told me that the sun was soon setting and that I must stay in my room now until the next morning. Under no circumstances was I to open my bedroom door she told me; no matter what. It must remain closed and I must remain in it.

I couldn't believe what was happening. Was I going to die in a few days? I turned on the Television to try to take my mind off it all and surprisingly I did eventually fall asleep. That was, until 1 a.m., when I was woken by the sound of tapping on my bedroom window. I told myself it had to be a tree branch or something. Then came a knock at my bedroom door, and I heard my grandpa's voice; "Are you okay? If you are scared, let me in and I will keep you company."

I was scared after the knocking on my window had woken me and I was relieved to hear the sound of my Grandpa's voice, so without thinking any more about it I rushed to the door to open it. But something wasn't right. As I glanced at one of the bowls of salt, I saw that it had turned black. And then I heard the sound again. 'Thump... Thump.' The tapping on my window came again. I fell to the floor and began to pray. I was so terrified. I did this until my clock said 7. 30 a.m. and it was morning.

Very slowly I opened my bedroom door and ran into my grandparents' room. They told me to pack a few things quickly and they drove me straight to the airport. Apparently, there were others who had escaped the grasp of the Hachi Saku Sama, as long as they had left the country and never returned. A few years later, my grandpa got sick, but he refused to allow me to go back to see him. After he died, he left strict instructions in his will – I was not to come for his funeral.'

Chapter Twenty-Two

'The Whistling People'

The Orang Bunian, or 'The Whistling People,' are said to be forest spirits who enchant and lead forest visitors astray. You can`t see them; but they can see you. They are also called the magical residents of the woods, according to Malaysian folklore. 'Orang Bunian' are said to be grouped under the family of the Jinn. It's said that if you hear shouting, singing, laughing or babbling in the woods, when you approach the source of the noise, you will not even see their shadows.

They are said to be responsible for making visitors get lost inside of forests, and they are believed to abduct humans when they feel like doing so. The Orang Bunian are often used as an explanation for why people have gone astray in the forest, and sometimes never been found. They are blamed for cases of missing children, and hunters, who are never seen again.

Their 'magic' is linked to their alleged ability to make themselves invisible. 'Bunian' comes from the word 'bunyi' meaning 'sound,' and refers to the fact that while you may hear them, you will never see them. Their domain is deep inside the forests, and humans who wish to pass through these places will apparently soon learn the error of their ways if they do not treat their home, the forest, with the utmost respect. They are masters of invisibility, time manipulation, and illusion, it is believed.

There is the story of Mohd Ghani, reported in the Malaysian Newspapers in 2008, as a 15-year-old boy who vanished for eight days in Gunung Tebu, a thick forested mountain region which rises to 1039 above sea level in Jerith, Malaysia. The Utusan Newspaper reported, "Mohd was found today in a place that had been repeatedly searched by the search party, triggering a mystery that has confounded police. Even Mohd wonders how the search team and volunteers and even his own mother did not see him when he was in that same area since he had been reported missing."

The boy himself said, "During the period the search parties and people were searching for me, I came across the search party. I heard my mother call but I couldn't do anything..."

It appears that he never left the area in which he had disappeared and was then subsequently found 8 days later; but he was there all the time. The searchers couldn't see him even though he could both hear them and see them, and he could clearly see his mother frantically searching for him.

The Newspaper wrote, 'State police Chief Lub Hussain expressed complete astonishment because the boy was found only 8 metres from the bridge on which he had last been seen.'

The Police Chief himself said, "I was quite surprised that after all the places we were looking for him, behold, he was at the centre of the public eye, by the river, and the funny thing is he's still in good health and showed no signs of fatigue."

More than 130 rescuers had been searching for 8 days for him, including the police, the army, and the People's Volunteer Corps. All the villagers nearby had joined in. None of them could find a trace of the missing boy, until eight days had passed, and then he was there, standing by the river; yet oddly, he was no longer wearing clothes; he had on just a towel, wrapped around his waist, and he was standing there, just gazing out over the river.

The boy, a boy scout, could not explain how he came to be wearing the towel, nor why he says he had been "hanging around the area the whole time," and yet no-one had been able to see him there. His mother, Zarodah Awangis, said that she believed he had been "hidden by the Goblins - the Orang Bunians."

Star Magazine of Malaysia quotes another local hiker, William Lee, who says that while people may scoff at those who believe in the existence of forest spirits or the supernatural, "Why do some people believe in God when they can't see proof of his existence? Often those who don't believe in supernatural spirits, and scoff at the suggestion, still won't dare walk through the forest or a cemetery at night!"

Another avid hiker called Nor Muzammil, said, "A few years ago, four of us were hiking and we could not get out of the forest. Usually from where we were, it would have taken around one hour to come to the forest edge, but for us, even after several hours, we seemed to be trapped inside. We were walking along the trail, which was an old mud-filled logging trail, which every hiker knows about, but suddenly, the trail had turned into a gravel path. We knew this wasn't right because we had hiked it many times before and there was no gravel path."

"That's when we decided to all say silent prayers, and we prayed "please, let us go home, and we apologise if we had offended anything in the forest," and we asked for forgiveness. It was only after we had done this that the trail opened up and we could see the familiar landmarks we knew again. For us, we believe now that the forest has its own inhabitants which we are not able to see. We know now that when we visit we must not be cocky, we must show respect for the rules."

Piek Lean also has a story, of the time something odd happened to her. Though she doesn't believe in 'forest spirits,' and has tried to rationalise what happened to her, she still can't explain it with any common sense answer. "Twice it happened to me in the forest that I knew very well. I walked in circles and I could not find my way out. When the searchers found me, the path was just there, right in front of me. Can I explain that? How could I have missed that? I don't know. Perhaps there are greater beings out there."

Trekking guide trainer Seelan Govindan, described the time he had been training a 'newbie' guide in the forest one day when he began to hear beautiful music coming from somewhere in the woods. "It was such an awesome sound and I know it was not a bird or an animal; yet the newbie had no reaction! She couldn't hear anything, yet the music was loud and beautiful and it seemed to come so close to us."

He said he felt like panicking but he tried to stay calm

and focus. He says he managed to maintain control of himself and get them out of the area calmly. "After that, as soon as I got the newbie out of that part of the woods, I went back. As soon as I stepped back into that section, everything was back to normal!"

Sarimah Yusuf is another hiker who had a terrible time when she was in the woods of Malaysia. She says she believes it all started when she innocently picked a strange flower as she neared the end of her hike.

"I felt strange as soon as I did it. I felt such sudden sadness, and yet I also didn't want to leave. I could hear a voice close to my ear. I felt tempted to follow the voice from below the hill. It was inviting me to follow it. Then I was crying hard. I didn't want to hear the voice any more. I felt as if I was entering a different world."

She had been with a party of hikers at the time and the leader of the hike, tour guide K. Ganesan, said that he remembered seeing her suddenly and inexplicably descending the steep hill by the abseiling rope, going extremely fast, as if she was in a blind panic.

"We heard a lady screaming and crying. We ran forward and saw it was the same lady who had roped down fast. We found her sitting at the base of a tree with both of her hands clutching her ears. Her head was down and she was shaking uncontrollably. We tried to calm her down and we tried to get her to walk with us. She was afraid of something we couldn't see but she said it was following us. As we led her out of the woods her fear changed to hysterical laughter. In our opinion she had become possessed by 'something,' says the guide.

Srimah says that her strange experience didn't end when she was led out of the woods. "That night I could still hear the voice screaming in my head."

Dr. Ong Hean-Tatt, an investigator of the paranormal in Malaysia, relates the strange case of 'The Lost Boys.' The story began on a typical weekend, at a busy tourist spot known as Fraser hill, a tourist highland spot in Malaysia, in June 2005. It was always busy there, being an excellent place for hiking, and among the tourists this day was a group of families from Singapore. There were two brothers and one cousin along with one of their fathers who was accompanying them that day as they went to hike there. The boys wanted to trek Bishop's Trail, and the father said he would wait for them at the end of the trail, which was about an hour's hike away. He would then take them for lunch afterwards he said. The teenage boys were confident of hiking it alone, because one of them was in the scouts. So they set off, with the agreement that they would meet the adult at the end of the route.

However, the hour deadline came and went, and there was no sign of the boys, and the father began to worry. Another hour passed by, and now he had become frantic. He reported the boys missing, and this saw the start of a five-day long search for the missing boys. Within hours, both the police and the army were called in to help look for the boys, but they had no luck finding them on the short trail. They found no trace of the boys at all.

A troop of senior scouts were brought in, as they'd been

previously successful in finding another group of hikers who had gone missing on the same trail. Before these scouts began their search, they prayed to the guardian spirits of the forest for help. Then, one of the scouts placed a lit cigarette down into the earth and waited.

The smoke from the cigarette started to drift toward the direction of a part of the forest which had been closed due to an earlier landslide. That part of the forest had been cordoned-off because it was not safe anymore, and so it seemed unlikely that anyone would be beyond the restricted area. However, the scouts followed the direction of the smoke and went inside the cordoned-off part of the forest, and before long, they found the lost boys. They were exhausted, but alive and without any injury. What they told the scouts however, was very strange.

They all said that as they were walking along, they began to hear strange music, and they followed the sound of it, until they reached an area that was unrecognisable yet astonishingly beautiful. They described the most vivid colors and such brightness and beauty, and they went into the place, as though they were entering another world altogether, and it wasn't until sometime later that they realised they were lost. It was as if they had been lured somewhere.

The scouts who found them thought this was particularly strange, because the area they were describing was nothing but mud because of the land slide. They also thought it very odd that the boys had managed to get to the part they had found them in too, because the scouts themselves had to abseil down a slope and they couldn't understand how the boys had got to where they had. The local people, who had joined in the search effort for the boys, were less surprised. They were certain that the forest spirits had played a trick on the visiting boys.

Dr. Ong Hean-Tatt, on describing the story, remarked that it's easy to put it down to a case of hiking without taking notice of the surroundings and getting lost quickly, as tiredness sets in perhaps, but what cannot be as easily explained away is that each boy attested to having heard the music and travelled into the strange world they had never seen before.

A.R. Amiruddin is a journalist with 25 year's experience. He's also been a keen hiker and mountaineer all of his life. "You may call it superstition, but the spirits of the mountain and forests do exist," he says. "They are the Penunggu; the guardian spirits of these places, and now, I always give due respect when 'trespassing' in these places. There are taboos to observe. I know; because I went through this mysterious journey. In the Cameron Highlands of Pahang, I was under the spell of these spirits. It was during my climb when I was descending alone. I found myself going round in a circle. It was clear within the circle, which was surrounded by plants in flower. I could not see any other path to get out by. I was trapped. I had no sense of time; my mind was blank."

"There was just silence and calm, until two other members of the mountaineering team arrived from their descent. We were on a trek of five days. They asked me what I was doing. I told them to join me. They knew something was terribly wrong; my face was white, my behaviour and body language totally out of the norm, and they said later that my voice was very forceful. They had to physically drag me out of the circle."

"None of us spoke for over an hour after that as we continued our descent. At the base, they told me what had happened. I had escaped from the clutches of the spirits. It was on this same expedition that another member saw a lake where none of us could. A different member believed that someone was following her but whenever she turned around there was no-one there. She heard the footsteps though.."

"This wasn't my first experience. In the 1980's I was riding my motorbike going to a friend's house late one night after the sun had set. I saw something in a black cloak flying toward the graveyard opposite the Army barracks. It was long-haired and flapping its arms like a bird but it was a female. I know; I saw it at close range and it was not a figment of my imagination. It happened. I remember cold sweat dripping from my body as the surge of fear swept over me. I was shaking uncontrollably, and in bed that night I developed a fever."

For the leader of the Harriers running club, this all brings back some disturbing memories of his own; or perhaps we should say, a disturbing lack of memories, because Hardip Singh, a 53-year-old paralegal, had undergone a similar experience of his own, which still to this day remains a complete blank for him. It had happened in the same woods.

"I remember making my way there, it was May 2012," he tells the Rakyat post, "and I was going to lay the trail for the run scheduled for that coming weekend. Then I can remember my wife embracing me as I lay on a stretcher having been brought down from the hike. Nothing comes to mind between that moment and when I arrived at the woods, or how I came to be found without clothes."

What transpired from the moment he stepped into the forest until he regained consciousness in the hospital is still a blank void, more than three years after the strange incident happened. "The police, I was told, were actively involved, which led to me being found, but to date, I cannot recollect what happened to me; nothing comes to mind. Everything I know about it today has been narrated to me after the event, by rescuers."

He adds that people have come up with various theories about his inexplicable experience, "Tales of how I could have offended the keepers of the forest, questions about how I ended up naked, how I survived without food and water; all remain unanswered and it is a big puzzle to me. Sometimes I have the chills when I try to remember things....I cannot remember meeting anyone else...."

The consensus of opinion locally however is that he did meet someone in the woods, or rather, he met the *Orang Bunian* who enchanted him and lead him away.

In July 2015, The Malaysia Star reported, "Lost Hiker Mystery; Did the *Orang Bunian* Kidnap Teo Lean?" The Malay Digest also reported on this mysterious case, of a person who had also gone missing in the forest. A man had disappeared on the popular Bukit Hatamas hiking trail in Cheras. Eight days into the search for him, one volunteer posted an update on facebook. Klang Hash wrote, "Strong evidence he is still alive! We found fresh blood stains, vomit, and footsteps deep in the woods. The missing man was a runner with the Harries local running group, which met weekly to go running and orienting on the trails throughout the forest.

The Fire and Rescue Department had led the initial search for him, alongside the Civil Defence Department, but they had called off the search after 10 days, after uncovering no sign of the missing man. He had last been seen by his wife, at home, when he told her he was going for an evening run in the woods. He never returned, and the next day, after she found his car in the car park by the woods with his cell phone inside, she called the police to report him missing.

They officially halted their search efforts on June 21, 2015, after combing a 10 km radius that turned up no leads. Teo Lean had seemingly disappeared, and despite more than 150 volunteers, 50 rescue personnel, and teams of tracker dogs, no trace of him had been found. It was at this point that search party co-coordinator Lieutenant Kil Hardial said they turned to help from Buddhist Mediums to try to find out where he could be.

"We have thoroughly combed all possible areas with the Civil Defence Department, the Fire and Rescue Department, and volunteers, but did not find any trace of him. We want them to point us in the right direction. We have exhausted every other possible means of finding him."

The Mediums were brought to the spot where the runner was last seen, and after prayers and meditation they all said that "the searchers must look north-west, from the foot of the hill." However, despite the search party taking their advice, they still didn't find him. The locals said it was because of the '*Orang Bunian*', or '*The Whistling People*,' who had whisked him away ... to another world that the searchers could not see.

In another very odd case in Malaysia, the newspaper headline said: 'A Malaysian Ferry Worker has called in 30 Bomos to solve the mystery of his missing son, believed to have been abducted by a ghost,' wrote The Straits Times on January 20th, 1956. 'The boy, Maksalmina Mohamed, 3 years old, went missing while playing near his home in Kampong Ringgit,' (4 hours

North of Kuala Lumpur.) 'Bomos' are Medicine Men. His mother and grandmother had been close-by the boy at the time he vanished.

At the nearest police station, they said that the father had reported the child missing several days ago, after he disappeared while out playing. The father of the missing boy had gathered a large group of villagers and they had searched everywhere in the area, from the small village, through the Woods to the sea, but no trace of the boy had been found. While the police were continuing the search for the boy, the Newspaper reported that all thirty Bomos (the medicine men) except for two of them, said that they believed the boy was still alive but was being kept hidden by the ghost who had kidnapped him.

In particular, some of the Bomos said that the boy was being held by what they called 'The Guardian of the Hill.' Almost all the Bomos agreed that if the little boy was not returned within the next 3 months, then he would never return.

The father and the villagers were inclined to believe the twenty-eight medicine men, who were telling the father that his boy had been taken by the ghost and that he was still alive but being held captive somewhere by the ghost. They all believed this was the most likely explanation. There appears to be no follow-up to the story, and so the fate of the little boy is not known, but the villagers all spoke of other incidents where this had happened before ....

~ ~ ~ ~

Russ Chastain, a hunting aficionado who writes on the subject of hunting, recalls an event that twenty-six years later still gives him shivers when he talks about it. He'd gone hunting with his Father. It was one of his first hunts as a teenage boy.

They had set up in separate trees and were now lying in wait for passing deer as the quiet afternoon turned to evening.

"All of a sudden I heard some noises; something was

moving nearby. I looked in that direction but all I could see was tree and bush moving that had been disturbed. It was still daylight."

Then, behind him, he heard rustling and saw more movement again in the bushes. "Somehow 'something' had got past me without being seen. Then suddenly, the quiet is shattered with the most blood-curdling scream; it was the most primal cries I'd ever heard.

"It seemed part-human, part-animal, and part-*spirit*, and completely evil. I couldn't pin it down. It was *ethereal.* Every hair on my body rose."

"Then it came again. My heart froze, my eyes bulged in their sockets, but it was hard to pin the source down; it was ethereal and *everywhere.*"

"I tried to shrink to invisibility. I was alone. It was getting dark," and there was something now between him and the safety of his truck.

"I held my gun tight, thinking how effective was it going

to be against something from hell, something I can't see? This was freaky. Guns don't kill demons. I got out of the tree and ran."

"What was even more freaky; my Dad had not heard it!" Back at his truck, when his father returned, hours later, and asked his son where he had been, Chastain in return asked his father why he had stayed there after the screaming.

His father had no idea what he was talking about – he had heard no screaming. To this day, the hunter has no idea what it was....

Chapter Twenty-Three

"Prepare to Die."

Next is another case where it seems that a spirit may have been in charge of a man's destiny; or at least, the foretelling of it; English aristocrat Lord Thomas Lyttelton was well known on the London social circuit in the 1770's for his 'wild ways.'

Indeed, he was more commonly referred to as 'The Wicked Lord Lyttelton. Educated at the elite private boarding school Eton and then Oxford University, he was a clever, talented and very charming man. He was also a notorious scandalous rake, who lived life to its fullest, excelling in extravagance and debauchery. He also had a passion for settling things by duels.

He was elected as an MP and sat in Parliament until he was unseated on the charge of bribery. After his father died, he became able to sit in parliament once more – this time taking his hereditary seat in the House of Lords.

He was the life and soul of any social gathering and famed for his entertaining character, as well as his scandalous one, so he was often talked about.

In 1772 Lyttleton married Apphia Peach, the wealthy widow of the governor of Calcutta, with a fortune of £20,000 – the equivalent today would be approximately £1.2 million. He soon lost interest in his new wife however, who many believed he had only married for her wealth, and after three months he returned to the social circuit of London for the gambling and the women. By early the following year, he had eloped to Paris for a wager of a hundred guineas, with the barmaid of Bolton's Inn at Hockerell. This was followed swiftly afterwards by Newspaper reports of another escapade when he got into a brawl over an actress in Vauxhall pleasure gardens.

He was a Georgian hellraiser, who excelled at gambling, fornication and drinking. He declared of himself, "My character is divided between an ardent desire of applause and a more than equal love of pleasure... I will freely own that my life has been marked with an extravagance of dissipation." One friend even said, "I think there is a mixture of insanity about him that drives him to perdition."

It was not this exuberant and debauched behaviour that garnered most attention however during the last week of his life – instead, it was a very strange tale that he himself told others. Lord Lyttelton told several people in his close circle of friends that something very unnerving had occurred on the night of November 24th, 1779, although he had shrugged the incident off. At the time, he was 35 years of age. It occurred when he was in his London home in Hill Street, Berkeley Square.

He said he was woken in the dead of night by what sounded like a bird flapping its wings on the curtains that enclosed his large four-poster bed. He opened his eyes and saw the shape of a bird which then transformed into a gaunt old lady, dressed head-to-toe in white and standing very close to his bed. She was withered and haggard and looked very ancient. She glared at him and pointed a finger at him accusingly before saying,

"Hear me now Lord Lyttelton, for I have come to tell you that you will be dead within three days. Prepare to die." Then she vanished.

Lyttelton was shaken to the core, and quickly called for his man-servant to come. The apparition had been so real that he knew this was no dream. The man servant the next morning could not help but tell his friends of the strange incident in the night, and they told others and soon the talk of the town was about the apparition and her deathly warning. Lyttelton himself went to his uncle Lord Wetcote, to tell him what had happened.

However, not one to let anything stop him from enjoying his wild ways, he managed to shake it from his mind and although he shared his experience with many of his close circle, he continued in his exuberant lifestyle. On the third day; the day of his predicted death, he took a group to a house he owned in Epsom, outside of London. With him were three sisters and several other friends. He joked with them that he was feeling very positive he would "bilk" the ghost; he believed he would evade it and remain victoriously alive.

That day, he and his cousin passed a graveyard, at which he remarked to his cousin. "You and I, who are gentlemen, shall live to a good old age.' That evening he held a dinner party where he appeared very cheerful and in apparent good health.

At a quarter past 11 that night, he climbed into bed, after requesting that his man-servant bring him a teaspoon so that he could eat some rhubarb. When his man-servant returned, Lord Lyttelton was lying on the floor, writhing in distress as though having a fit. Before the clock struck midnight, he was dead.

Even more strangely, Thomas Lyttleton seems to have not been the only one in his lineage to have received the most horrifying visitation from the supernatural realm. Indeed, a descendent, George Lyttleton also had a terrifying encounter in the very same Square, Berkeley Square, in London, a century later, in 1872.

This time, it was 'The Demon of fifty Berkeley Square,' who was later said to have claimed many lives; for few who saw it lived to tell the tale.

The address of 50 Berkeley Square was once the London home of a prime minister, and this was where, in 1872, aristocrat and politician Lord George Lyttleton stayed the night in the house for a bet. He set up a bed in the attic where he was to spend the night, to prove to others that he could withstand any supernatural onslaught from whatever it was that lived there. Despite not really believing in the rumours, he still took a shotgun with him for good measure, as if to ward off the demon by shooting it.

He later reported that during the night, an apparition appeared in the form of a swirling mass of mist, and he did indeed shoot it. In the daylight of the next morning, he found the attic to be completely empty. He reported that the upper floor of the house "was supernaturally fatal to body and mind."

This would in fact prove to be the case. Eight years later, n 1840, another aristocrat Sir Robert Warboys, was drinking with friends when he heard of the reputation of the house as a haunted location. Dismissing the stories as ludicrous, his friends in turn challenged him to stay the night in the house. Warboys eagerly took them up on their bet, thinking it would be great fun and his scepticism should be proved right.

His friends insisted however that he must take his gun to the house and keep it in the bedroom, where he was to stay alone, and the caretaker of the property advised him that he must ring the bell in the bedroom should he need assistance at any time during that night.

The caretaker and his friends waited downstairs, sitting all together in a group for protection, and Sir Robert was left alone in the bedroom above.

All was quiet until at about a quarter to one in the morning, when the bell from his bedroom suddenly sounded, and the men ran quickly up to the bedroom, hearing a gunshot as they ran up the stairs.

Pushing open the door they found Sir Robert on the floor, his pistol still smoking in his hand but no physical entity in the room with him. Sir Robert however was dead. When they found him, his face was contorted in a death-mask grimace of terror. He had, they declared, died from fright.

Many years later, two sailors from the naval base of Portsmouth were in town on leave and noticing a 'To Let' sign hung outside the house, they decided it would make a great place to stay for free digs for the night instead of having to pay for a hotel room. They broke into the house and found all the rooms empty save for a top floor bedroom with a bed, and having had a long night of drinking, they quickly got into the bed to get some sleep.

One of the sailors however, Edward Blunden, felt oddly nervous and too unsettled to go to sleep. For some reason he lay restless and awake in bed, as his companion Robert Martin snored soundly. Suddenly Edward heard the sound of footsteps coming toward the closed bedroom door, and very scared, he quickly woke his friend up. Something large, dark and shapeless was entering the room. It flew at Edward, attacking him, while Robert managed to flee in terror from the room.

Spotting a policeman on patrol in the street, he ran to him and told him his friend needed their help; that he was being attacked, and they both ran back to the house.

But they were too late. The broken body of Edward lay on the stairs of the basement, his neck broken, and his dead face fixed in an expression of horror.

Reportedly, in later years, the maid of a family who had rented the house without knowledge of its past, died in hospital after being found crumpled on the floor, whimpering: "Don't let it touch me."

She described what she saw as "too horrible;" then died quickly afterwards in St Georges Hospital...

~ ~ ~ ~

A manuscript was discovered in County Waterford, Ireland, written sometime in the 1700's by a Lady Betty Cobbe, recording the very strange death of her grandmother Lady Beresford. It is the story of 'The

Beresford Ghost.' The story had been passed down through the family for generations and found its way into the archive at the Armagh County Museum.

The story goes that one morning, Sir Marcus Beresford was surprised to find his wife arriving for breakfast looking white as a ghost and with a sombre black ribbon tied around one of her wrists. He asked his wife was wrong, but she refused to tell him. All that she would say was that from now on, she would always wear her black ribbon. Despite him trying to press her for an explanation, she steadfastly refused to say any more, and eventually he had to drop it, even though he could get no sense from her and could see no reason why she would be wearing this black ribbon, which seemed to have appeared from no-where. He could think of nothing to explain his wife's odd behaviour.

Her strange behaviour continued, when she asked, rather urgently, if the morning post had yet arrived. This led him to speculate that her behaviour must surely be due to the expectation of something very important coming in the mail; but what, he wondered?

263

He asked his wife if she were expecting an important letter, to which she replied that she was; "I'm expecting to hear that Lord Tyrone is dead."

Lady Beresford and Lord Tyrone had been born in Ireland. They were not related by birth, but both being orphaned at the same time at an early age, they were given into the care of the same person. Under the care of this guardian, both accepted the principles of a religion called 'Deism.' This is a belief in the existence of a supreme being, specifically of a creator, who does not intervene in the Universe. After this guardian died, they were then placed into the care of another guardian, who had a different belief system based more on traditional religion. The two orphans, now in their teen years, made a firm pact.

They promised each other that whoever died first, they would return to the one still living and reveal to them which religious belief was best – Deism, which is more along the lines of Atheism, or a traditional religion such as Catholicism, with its belief in God and the afterlife. If they returned to the one still living, it would prove that there was a Heaven and an Afterlife. So they vowed that whoever died first, they would try to return.

Sometime later, the girl married Sir Tristram and she became Lady Beresford. In turn, the boy also married, and the two families enjoyed a close friendship, often spending several weeks in each other's company.

When Lady Beresford came down for breakfast that morning wearing her black ribbon and told her husband she was expecting a letter that morning, a letter duly arrived, and it bore the terrible news that her beloved brother was indeed dead.

Lady Beresford never spoke again about her ribbon, and life went on. Her husband died four years later, and she went on to marry again, having two daughters and then a son in her late forties. While still recovering in bed from the birth of her son at home, the local clergyman came to visit her. They were close, and he expressed his joy that she had given birth to a healthy boy at the age of 47 – and on the day of her birthday too. Lady Beresford quickly corrected him; telling him that she was 48 today, not 47.

He insisted however, that this was not the case – on hearing of the birth of her son, he said he had checked in the Parish register to find out her age. There was a long silence, after which Lady Beresford declared: "Sir, you have signed my death warrant."

She then asked the clergyman to leave. Lady Cobb, her friend who was staying with her, noted his rather embarrassed departure and he told her what had happened upstairs. Lady Cobb found her friend's behaviour most odd, and after the vicar had left, she went upstairs to ask Lady Beresford what had happened.

Lady Beresford solemnly told her friend. She revealed that one night, many years ago, her beloved brother Lord Tyrone had appeared to her in her bedroom, and he had told her he was now dead. He told her that her husband would die, but that she would marry again and have two daughters and a son, then she would die at the age of 47. Given that, or so she thought, she had reached the age of 48 today, his prophesy had not come true; that was, until the clergyman told her today she had just turned 47.

To allay any doubt in her friend's scepticism about this supposed appearance of her dead brother's apparition, she told her friend that the reason she wore the black ribbon around her wrist was because she had asked her dead brother to prove to him that he was real – to which he had touched her wrist. The hand that touched her wrist was ice-cold and where the icy fingers touched her skin it had caused her skin to wither. The ghost of her brother then told her never to let anyone see what had happened to her wrist. That was why she wore the black ribbon – to cover up her withered flesh. All of his predictions had come true – except for her own death.

Her friend, seeing that she was over-wrought with anxiety, tried to reassure her that this couldn't be true and that she was just tired and over-emotional from having just given birth, and her friend advised her to rest and try to take a nap. Lady Cobb left the room, telling her friend to ring the bell beside her bed if she needed her.

About an hour later, Lady Cobb was sitting downstairs in the lounge dozing herself, when she suddenly heard the light ringing of the bell from Lady Beresford's bedroom. Quickly getting up, she went upstairs, but when she entered Lady Beresford's bedroom, she found her lying dead in bed. Unable to resist and so intrigued by her friend's story about the ribbon, she could not stop herself from untying it and looking at her friend's wrist – sure enough, the flesh on Lady Beresford's wrist had withered away...

~ ~ ~ ~

The oldest journal still in publication, The Scots Magazine, first issued in 1739, wrote of a very strange incident that occurred in 1761.

Five women were returning from collecting wood near Ventimiglia in northern Italy, when suddenly one of them cried out and dropped to the ground, dead. Her friends were terrified by what they saw.

Her clothes and even her shoes were apparently torn into shreds and scattered all around her. Her wounds were horrific; her skull was visible, her intestines hanging out, and most of her internal organs ruptured.

Her femur had been torn from its socket and the flesh of her hip and thigh torn off.

The account was recorded in the French Academy of Sciences by Dr M. Morand. He wrote that there was no blood at the scene, nor any sign of her missing flesh.

Chapter Twenty-Four

Killer in the House.

The house was of evil abode. Replete with disturbing noises, foul smells, and an ever-present ominous air. It had a life of its own. It was located on Coxwell Road in the Ladywell district of Birmingham, England. When Mr. and Mrs. Pell learned they were to be its new occupants, they knew none of this. All they knew was that they were overjoyed to be leaving their own house, which had been condemned as unfit to live in, and they were moving to this newly decorated home in a quiet street and were being asked to pay a very low rent. It was wonderful news. It was cheap, close to transport links, schools and all the local conveniences were right on their doorstep.

Perhaps they did hear some of the local rumours though — for before they moved in, they asked a priest to bless the house. Had they heard of the local gossip — of a terrible sulphur stench reported by the previous residents? Did they hear talk of the strange noises that came from the house at night? Whatever they did hear, it seems that they believed a Priest would be sufficient to put to bed any rumours or gossip about the house and after all, it was too good an opportunity to miss. Their five children couldn't wait to move in and there was plenty of space for them all.

Father Francis Etherington duly blessed their new home and they moved in immediately afterwards. It was the weekend and all the children were therefore home free to roam the house and play games. But it was this weekend that it all began for them. On the second night in the house, Mr and Mrs Pell were awoken rudely by the sound of a slamming door. They both sat bolt upright in bed, listening for further sounds and heard a door being opened slowly, quietly, followed by a resounding bang as it slammed closed. Then they heard a door open again and close once more, but this time gently.

Their new baby was sleeping between them in bed. Mr Pell said to his wife that a window must have been left open and the wind was catching the door, although both of them had heard the distinct sound of a door knob being turned. The wind was also not capable of the whispering sounds they could also hear as Mr Pell reached out to feel for the bedside lamp to turn on the light.

He got out of bed and made his way downstairs to look for an open window. Standing in the kitchen, he was baffled by the strange sound of scratching and scuttling, coming from above his head on the ceiling. As he looked up, there was a sudden heavy thud, too big of a sound for it to be a rat or mouse. Then there was just silence. Eventually, he returned to the bedroom.

The following night, and the night after that, and every night, disturbances became normality for the family. The parents of course checked whether the bangs and slamming doors could be the fault of their young children, playing pranks, but each night the children were all found to be sleeping when the banging began, and continued, with none of the children ever leaving their beds. The parents had to admit to each other, that there was no obvious earthly cause for these bangs and slamming doors. It was not the wind, it was not mice or rats, it was not their children, it was not either of them. It came from all parts of the house. There was also no explanation for the eerie whispering voices they heard in the dead of night, every night.

There were some strange eccentricities to the noises. Each night, at exactly the same time, tapping would come from the ceiling of the kitchen. The room above it was unoccupied. In this room, the temperature wildly fluctuated. When the mother was cleaning it one day, she said it felt as though icy fingers were running down her back.

She told her husband, of course, but they both decided that since no real harm had been done to her, or any of the family, other than scare the wits out of them, they didn't want to move out of their otherwise idyllic house, which was such an improvement from their old house that had been condemned as unfit to live in. This was, until they woke up one morning to find their baby daughter lying dead in bed between them.

There were no marks on her body; nothing to explain how she could have ended up dead. She had not been ill in any way. She had been perfectly healthy. Neither parent had rolled over onto her and suffocated her. The doctor could find no obvious cause of death.

They buried their child that week, and returned home again, in dreadful grief but with no choice but to carry on their lives as best they could, for the sake of their other children. They were given the verdict of accidental death of their youngest child, and there was nothing more they could do. Life carried on, but it was not long before the parents began to notice a terrible odour in the house, of something decaying, of something that felt ancient, although they could find no source.

A few nights passed and then one evening, before the children went to bed, four-year-old Sammy asked his parents; "Did baby go with the white dog?"

The parents looked at each other, confused by his question.

"What white dog?" his mother asked.

"The white dog that comes and sits on my bed!" Sammy replied.

"When did you last see the dog?" his father asked.

"The night baby left he was sitting on baby's face," replied their young son. His mother became hysterical. His father could not calm her. The next day he went to the police. The priest too was summoned to the house.

The police undertook an investigation in the house, searching for a white dog, but of course they found no dog. The Priest conducted a cleansing of the house, throwing holy water into each room. In the room above the kitchen he heard the tapping that the mother heard every day at the same time. When the priest left, he said he feared he had not removed the presence from the house; that he did not think he was able to. He advised them to leave.

The family did not leave however; they still stayed, despite the tragedy that had taken place. The doors still slammed, the ancient smell of terrible decay lingered and grew, and the hushed eerie whispers would now follow them around the house. One evening when the mother was upstairs alone and her husband was in the kitchen shaving, he became more aware than usual of the whispering voices. They came around him intensely, menacingly, and he rushed to find his wife, filled with an overwhelming need to make sure she was ok.

He found her standing at the top of the stairs. She was standing in a peculiar manner. Her head was thrown back and her entire body was rigid, in an impossibly uncomfortable way. Her eyes were wide open, her mouth was stretched wide, and her hands were clenching and unclenching at her sides. She was trying to scream but no sound was coming out. He tried to reach her, to comfort her, but there was some form of invisible barrier preventing him, stopping him from getting to her, until he used all of his strength to pull himself up the stairs, gripping the handrail and pushing up against the invisible force until he reached her, at which piercing screams filled his ears. It was his wife's screams.

When he managed to sit his wife down and comfort her, she told him that she had heard the voices and they had got closer and closer to her; insistent voices, surrounding her. Her husband realized that the voices seemed to have been urging his wife, through fear, to throw herself down the stairs, and they had tried to prevent him from reaching her or hearing her screams for help. Only a 6th sense had made him rush to find her – only that had saved her, but next time, how could he expect to be so lucky? The voices had tried to kill her, they had killed his child. He could take no more loss. That night they finally left the house.

~ ~ ~ ~

Excerpt from Steph Young's

'An investigation into the Smiley Face Killers.'

On 12th June 2005 in Casnovia, Michigan, 22-year-old Todd Geib was last seen at a bonfire party. It was a marshy rural area. He left the party to walk back alone to his cousin's house, where he lived. He never made it back there. He called a friend at 12:51 a.m., but all he said was; "I'm in a field," before the phone call cut off. When the friend rang back, all the friend could hear was what sounded like the wind.

The area where he was last seen was thoroughly searched three times. During one of the searches, as many as 1,500 volunteers searched the area. He was not found.

When his body was discovered three weeks later in a remote bed of water, his death was ruled as 'undetermined.' When a new autopsy was carried out, he was discovered to have been dead only 2-5 days, despite being missing for 3 weeks. In other words, he had been kept somewhere, alive, for approximately two and a half weeks prior to his death. Where he was found had been thoroughly searched at least 3 times.

When independent pathologist Dr. Sikirica was allowed access to the autopsy files, he concluded through forensic analysis that Todd had been dead only between two to five days; and most crucially his body was not in the condition it would be expected to be in and he had *no water* in his lungs; so, *he could not have drowned.* He had not been in the water for the twenty or so days he had been missing; he had been held or kept alive somewhere for approximately three weeks, before being taken to the creek. He had been placed into the water to make it look like he had drowned. Where had he been before this was done to him? What was done to him when he was held somewhere, by someone?

According to the couple who found Todd, he was "standing upright" in Obenhall Lake. It was reported; 'They remember it distinctly because "his head and shoulders were sticking out of the water." This is not how a person drowns, and this is not the sort of position a person will die in. It is as though he had been put into that position, deliberately, like a raised flag, like someone leaving a message, like someone taunting those who would eventually have to retrieve his body. Said journalist Piehl at the time; "These drowning mysteries, they defy logic."

Dr. Sikirica's opinion, that Todd did not die in the pond but was later placed into the pond, was backed up by 200 other forensic examiners when he presented the strange case at an international convention of Medical Examiners. There was no mistaking that this was not normal.

Piehl said of the cases she investigated, "A lot of people have asked me, who is doing this? Whoever had Todd is a sick individual. I think we're going to find a dark human being, of a kind we haven't met yet." But the odds are, it's more than one person. As the cases turn into a heavy pile of files, it will become very clear that this is not the work of one killer.

Forty more boys had died at their hands, the detectives believed. The phrase 'The Smiley Face Killers' was derived from the claim by detective Gannon that graffiti was being found at or near the bodies, of a 'smiley face' sometimes with devil horns.

Patrick McNeill was 21 when he walked out of a bar in New York City on a cold night in February 1997. He told his friends he was taking the subway back to Fordham University where he was studying, but he never made it back there.

His body was found in the water at Owl's Head Water Pollution Plant near a Brooklyn pier almost two months later. His body was found face-up, which is not the usual position for a person who has drowned. The Pathologist stated he was *not drunk* when he died of drowning, but some very concerning questions arose. According to Det. Gannon, as the young man exited the Bar he'd been drinking in, The Dapper Dog in uptown Manhattan, he appeared very drunk; so much so that he was bending over in the street as though he needed to vomit. He seemed very uncoordinated.

He attempted to walk off down the street, stumbling along, and as he did so a double-parked car began to move beside him. Patrick stopped again as though he was about be sick, stumbled and fell over. The car beside him stopped. When Patrick managed to recover and pick himself back up, the car began to follow him again. He was found more than forty days later, dead in the river. He was found face-up and partially clothed.

Interestingly, 'a couple' were said to have been in the car following Patrick McNeill before he vanished. Of course, couples are less likely to arouse suspicion. And yet why would a woman be involved in this kind of thing?

At Patrick McNeill's inquest the Pathologist noted a possible ligature mark around the man's neck but this was not followed up by the police. Another renowned independent Forensic Pathologist, Dr. Cyril Wecht when reviewing the case for journalist Kristie Piehl stated, "There's no way this man is accidentally going to fall into a body of water, (and) the fly larvae (was found) to have been laid in the groin area. It's an indoor fly—not an outdoor fly. So, we have a body that was *already dead* before it was placed in the water...I would call it a homicide, yes."

In other words, the young man had been kept alive for an extended period of time again, prior to being found in the water; long enough for indoor larvae to settle on his body. He had been kept alive somewhere, indoors. Then he had been taken to the river and placed in it. The city medical examiner had ruled Patrick's death an 'accidental drowning.' Gannon said, "He was stalked, abducted, held for an extended period of time, murdered, and disposed of. They're psychopaths....they have no remorse."

Gannon's team believed that the black 'decomposition' noted in the city examiner's report was in actuality 'charring.' Gannon believed McNeill had been burnt from the head down to mid-torso, with something like a blow-torch. From the possible 'ligature mark,' Gannon's team suggested McNeill could have been bound in a chair, tied by the neck, restrained and tortured, as his back appeared to have no charring to it, only his front.

A few months before Patrick McNeill's disappearance Larry Andrews had come into New York City by train with a large group of friends, from their home town in Westchester County. It was New Year's Eve and they were excited to be joining the celebrations in the big city. However, Larry never made it to Times Square.

The group arrived at Grand Central Station and went to a Bar called Houlihan's close-by. Then they began a bar-hop. At some point during this, one moment Larry was suddenly gone. He was last known to have been on 42nd Street. Then he simply vanished. 6 weeks later, on the 12th February 1997 he was found. His body was floating in the Bay Ridge River, off Owl's Head Park. His body was not far from where Patrick McNeill's body would later be found. He was still wearing the winter clothing he'd set out in. His wallet with money inside was still on his body.

"He disappeared off the face of the Earth," his Father said. "There was no reason for him to walk to the water all the way on the West side. I think he met up with someone."

His sister said, "He was last seen running in his T-shirt heading west away from the train station. He gave someone a Yankees cap - which he did not have when he left Brewster. And he was no longer wearing the black turtleneck, his sweatshirt or his jacket."

Larry was found in the water off Owl's Head Park. Patrick McNeill was found close-by at Owl's Head Water Pollution Plant. Josh Szostak's parents found a severed owl's head on their doorstep.

Josh Szostak had been spending the evening of December 22nd 2007 celebrating a friend's birthday in a bar called the Bayou Cafe. Later his friends said there was nothing about Josh's behavior that night which caused them any concern; nothing stood out or alerted them to what was to come.

While Josh was inside the bar on North Pearl Street in downtown Albany, New York, his evening was captured on security surveillance footage. He was enjoying his night, drinking beer, listening to music and having fun. It's thought he had three beers; not an exceptional number, particularly for a young man his size. He was over 6 ft and not a lightweight. He was a fit young man and was enrolled as a student at the local college. That night, he certainly didn't appear to be falling down drunk or stumbling around. Everything was normal, for a while.

None of Josh's friends can explain what happened shortly after midnight, or why Josh and a friend went outside. The most logical explanation is that they wanted some fresh air; the bar inside was packed with young people. A street camera located adjacent to the bar captured him as he exited the bar with his friend. It's not clear footage; the quality of it is quite grainy, and of course it's old now, but it is available to watch on YouTube.

Josh and his friend stand outside directly in front of the bar for a couple of minutes talking, and then his friend leaves, presumably going home. His other friends are still inside the bar. The footage shows that Josh then suddenly appears to become very hot. It looks like he takes off not only his jacket but a jumper too.

Josh then, appears to be suddenly very hot on a cold night in December, but it isn't just that; he can be seen stumbling, and suddenly uncoordinated. He looks like he is struggling to sort out his jacket and jumpers. At one point he attempts to put his jacket back on and it looks as though he is about to put it on back to front, until he straightens it out and manages to get it on. He is glancing around at people and back toward the bar entrance, but he doesn't appear to be worried or necessarily anxious or scared at all, he just looks really out of it. As the CCTV images continue, he walks from the left side of the screen, across in front of the bar, past the entrance door, and comes to a halt on the right-hand side of the screen.

Outside the bar, after getting his jacket back on, he now seems to gather himself together and begins to walk off. He exits from the screen on the right-hand side and disappears from view. Inexplicably, he was not seen on any more surveillance cameras. He should have been, if he continued walking, because there were other cameras on the sidewalks along his route, but it was as though he simply vanished. Of course, no-one knew he'd gone missing just yet.

In an eerily and chilling replication of the disappearance of Patrick McNeill, according to Cardinalpoints online Josh's father said, "A vehicle was seen on camera several times driving past the Cafe my son was in, prior to his disappearance. Cameras then spotted the car later at two locations, after a vehicle was stolen from the Dept. of Environmental Conservation on the port. After this vehicle left the parking lot there, it drove to the most southern part of the port. This part of the port is the only area not covered by cameras. Two cameras spotted it during this time and the vehicle was seen driving past the Cafe. The vehicle that was following was abandoned by the driver."

The search for Josh continued for weeks, but there was no sign of him and no leads to follow. It was to be four long months until he was found, on April 22nd 2008, dead in the Hudson River in the Coxsackie area, about 20 miles away.

The ruling of 'accidental death' also didn't explain why, on the one-year anniversary of Josh's death, when his parents returned from visiting his grave, they found a message on their ansaphone. When they listened to it, it was their son crying for his Mom.

The message had been pre-recorded, of course, because their son was now dead. Someone, perhaps more than one, had made that recording while their son was still alive. His killers took pleasure in making that recording. His killers enjoyed sending that recording to his parents.

Larry Andrews was found off Owl's head. Patrick McNeill was found at Owl's head water pollution plant, close to Larry. Josh's parents were sent a severed Owl's head after their son was found dead. It was left on their doorstep....

Tracking the Smiley Face Killers ....
Scores of young men have vanished without a trace, only to be found dead weeks or months later, in remote rivers or creeks, shallow ponds or canals, in areas that search parties have searched multiple times before; then later their bodies are discovered there, as though they have been placed there deliberately to be found.

"They go directly into the shallow water. And then they are all gone….. no ghost, no memories…..as if they never lived in the first place. And then they stay there; awake and afraid."

"The evil is rampant and deep and widespread. He was tortured, taken to the river and killed. Then his body was 'positioned."

"Loaded in cargo van. Paid in dollars green."

"We take what we need and leave. Understand this: This is necessary. Life feeds on life feeds on life feeds on death feeds on life."

"To murder a man was an act of the greatest devoutness.'

"This is what they did to my son. Someone killed my son. Before Henry died, he was pleading to someone who dropped him in the dark… Henry paid for you to learn the lesson… that morning, he had no idea that he was going to die…"

There is something very sinister happening to college-age men. It has been going on since the early '90's, and quite probably since before then. It isn't stopping; it appears to be escalating.

Young men attending college are going missing; the numbers are rising as they disappear in what can only be described as the most sinister and inexplicable circumstances. Then they are found dead; always in water, often very shallow water. Very often however, they have not drowned.

'He is screaming, pleading and growling in raw, animalistic agony. In the background, a voice interrupts his screams and calmly tells him, in a cold, emotionless, detached voice, "Stop it."

"I couldn't get through to him. He couldn't talk. He couldn't tell me where he was. 8 minutes into the call there was suddenly this ghastly screaming. I started crying."

Continued in <u>An Investigation into The Smiley Face Killers</u>

Excerpt from 'People Missing in The Woods; True Stories of Unexplained Disappearances.'

Another very unsettling case of a man who went into the woods and never came back, happened when he was working as part of a four-man survey crew. It took place in Harris County, Georgia. It was January 25th, 2002 when 20-year-old

Christopher Carlton Thompkins said 'Goodbye' to his mum and left the home he shared with her to drive to work. What his mother could never have imagined was that this would be the last time she would ever see her son.

"I need closure," she told the Ledger Enquirer, after six years had passed with no sign of her son. "I need to know what happened that day, and where my son's body is."

Her son was last seen in a wooded area between Warm Springs Road and Georgia 85 near County Line Road. His mother relates what she knows:

"He left home about 8:10 a.m. He parked his car at work and drove to the job-site with the surveyor he worked for. At the time, I was also employed by the surveyor's family as their baby-sitter. He worked that morning with three other employees in a lightly wooded area off County Line Road. All the workers were about 50 feet from each other, walking in the same direction."

"Around 1 p.m. the surveyor phoned his wife to inform her that Christopher was missing. One of Christopher's co-workers said Christopher was walking in the same direction as the others. When he looked away and then looked back, Chris was gone."

His mother didn't immediately know her son had mysteriously vanished. "I was not informed until 4:15 p.m." She adds that she was not allowed to file a missing person's report until 24 hours had passed.

In the meantime, she says they organised their own search, and she says they combed every inch of the area he was working in when he vanished.

"What we found was puzzling, and what did not make any sense in light of what Christopher's co-workers told authorities, was we found one of his boots, his work tools, a blue fibre from his pants and 12 cents on the ground near the items."

"The statements by his employer and co-workers indicated that they believed Christopher just walked off the job site without telling anyone. His other boot was found several months later, miles from the original boot, on some property off I-85." His second boot was found by the owner of the property.

His mother does not believe her son would simply walk away from a job-site, in winter, wearing one or no boots.

His employer apparently said that in the days prior to her son's disappearance he had been acting "strangely." His employer however did not offer any specific details to elaborate on this, and his mother said she was not convinced.

"I saw him every day – he lived with me! There was no strange behaviour, nor any distress."

The Ledger Enquirer wrote in an update a few months afterwards, 'Christopher Carlton Thompkins did not disappear without a trace, but a trace of the 20-year-old is all searchers found when he was last seen Jan. 25, 2002.'

The most obvious explanation about what happened is that hypothetically his co-workers were behind his disappearance. An argument that quickly developed into an altercation. Christopher was somehow flung against the fence, which nicked fibres from his clothing and left them behind when he vanished. He was lifted up somehow during the fight, causing his loose change to fall out of his pocket, he ended up on the other side of the fence, ran, fled, lost a boot, and so on, and yet doesn't that seem a great feat for an assailant or group of assailants to achieve?

How did his boot end up 1.2 miles away? Why was no blood found at the scene? Where did his body go? And, let's just suggest that it was hypothetically the co-workers, the biggest question is, why would they make up such a story about him literally vanishing, within seconds, while he visibly standing among them?

It sounds too fantastical, too otherworldly to believe; or, did something so strange happen to him that they really cannot put it into words?

Was he fleeing something? Something the others did not see? Was he taken right before their eyes...?

~ ~ ~ ~

In 2002, the strange story of what happened to Todd Sees began to circulate. Just after 5am on August 4th, Todd left his rural home in Northumberland, Pennsylvania to go up into the nearby mountain to do some pre-season deer scouting. As he left home, he told his family he would be home by midday.

When he didn't return his concerned wife alerted authorities, knowing it was completely out of character for him not to return as he'd said he would. By 2pm, a search party had been organized. The State police and a couple hundred local volunteers began to search for him. Quickly they discovered his four-wheeler at the top of the mountain, but search dogs could find no scent to go on.

The search carried on for two days, from top to bottom of the mountainous area. On the second day a break came; something was seen in a thick brush area beside a pond, very close to the family home. The search party spent half an hour hacking at the brush to get to it. What they found was Todd Sees' body, virtually naked. He was wearing just his underwear. When he'd left two days before, he'd been fully dressed in outdoor clothing and boots.

His body was not bloated; it was emaciated. Immediately there were concerns. That would not be the usual condition to find a body in. It got stranger. Though many locals claimed afterward there was nothing unusual about the incident, others, including Emmy award winning investigative journalist Linda Molten Howe, and Peter Davenport of the National UFO Reporting Centre, believed there was a lot more to the case. They pointed to the fact that the area had been previously searched, and yet the tracker dogs had not been able to pick up his scent at all. Why?

This led to speculation that his body could not have been there when the area was searched but was perhaps placed there later. His body was found in a thickly forested spot, so difficult to access that it led many to believe he could not have gone there voluntarily, by his own volition, if the searchers themselves had to hack their way into it to retrieve him. But who or what had taken him in there if it was such a difficult area to get to? Even odder, one of his missing boots was later found; high up in a tree a mile from where his vehicle was found, and no-where near his body. People wanted to know how the boot could have got up there....

Continued in <u>People Missing in the Woods: True Stories of Unexplained Disappearances</u>

I hope you have enjoyed this book. If you have enjoyed it, perhaps you would be kind enough to leave a review, thank you so much, Steph '

Please go to <u>StephYoungAuthor.com</u> if you would like to stay up to date with new releases.

I have a Podcast: Unexplained Mysteries with Steph Young on iTunes & Patreon.com Steph Young Podcast **https://www.patreon.com/stephyoungpodcast**

Other Books by Steph Young:

Stalked in the Woods,

Demons: True Stories,

True Stories of Real Time Travelers, Haunted Asylums

Creepy Tales of Unexplained Disappearances

Panic in the Woods

Unexplained Disappearances & Mysterious Deaths

Predators in the Woods

Desolating Spirits

https://www.amazon.com/Steph-Young/e/B00KE8B6B0/

Made in the USA
Middletown, DE
28 March 2019